AND THE WORD
BECAME HISTORY

D1736250

AND THE WORD BECAME HISTORY

Messages Forged in the Fires

of Central American Conflict

MEDARDO ERNESTO GÓMEZ

Translated by Robert F. Gussick

Augsburg   Minneapolis

AND THE WORD BECAME HISTORY
Messages Forged in the Fires of Central American Conflict

Interior design: James F. Brisson
Cover design: Lecy Design

Library of Congress Cataloging-in-Publication Data

Gómez, Medardo Ernesto, 1945–
　[Sermons. English. Selections]
　And the Word became history : messages forged in the fires of Central American conflict / Medardo Ernesto Gómez : translated by Robert F. Gussick.
　　p. cm.
　Translated from Spanish.
　ISBN 0-8066-2574-0
　1. Lutheran Church—Sermons.　2. Sermons, English—Translations from Spanish.　3. Sermons, Spanish—Translations into English.
　I. Title.
BX8066.G593S47213　　1992
252'.041—dc20　　　　　　　　　　　　　　　　　　　91-23448
　　　　　　　　　　　　　　　　　　　　　　　　　　　　　　CIP

The paper used in this publication meets the minimum requirements of American National Standard for Information Sciences—Permanence of Paper for Printed Library Materials, ANSI Z329.48-1984.　　　　　　　∞™

Manufactured in the U.S.A.　　　　　　　　　　　　　　　　AF 9-2574

96　95　94　93　92　1　2　3　4　5　6　7　8　9　10

CONTENTS

FOREWORD BY MARTIN E. MARTY   7

TRANSLATOR'S PREFACE BY ROBERT F. GUSSICK   9

INTRODUCTION
Medardo Ernesto Gómez, A Man of Destiny   26

1   The Mission of the Church as the Prophetic Voice of God   31

2   The Church of Jesus Christ Must Preach the Truth   39

3   The Church of Jesus Christ Will Receive Eternal Glory   47

4   Jesus Christ Is the Conqueror of All Temptations   55

5   Jesus Christ Is the History of Salvation   67

6   Jesus Christ Gives Us His Friendship in the Gospel   73

7   Walking Together Is Giving Testimony to Jesus Christ   81

8   The Holy Spirit Unites Christians in Joy   89

9   Jesus Christ Is the Conscience for Communal Action   99

FOREWORD

A generation ago the walls of campus ministry offices or seminary dormitory rooms bore pictures of contemporaries from the northern worlds: Dietrich Bonhoeffer, Pope John XXIII, Martin Luther King, Dorothy Day, and the like. Today they are more likely to bear those of Christians from the southern worlds: Mother Teresa, Desmond Tutu, Oscar Romero, Beyers Naude, Dom Helder Camera, and their like. Make room for another: that of Medardo Ernesto Gómez, the author of the messages in this book, messages capably introduced by Robert Gussick, the pioneer in Lutheran work in Central America, a man for whom the designation "gringo" never fit. In the least.

But: to Bishop Gómez. His is a little flock, a lonely band of evangelical Lutherans in an environment once hostile, still strange. His is a voice for justice and mercy in an El Salvador whose powers know little about justice and whose anti-powers show little of mercy. Within these environs and between these voices, Medardo Gómez, a friend in his youth of the assassinated Catholic Romero but who heard a parallel gospel call in Lutheranism, is credible when he speaks of justice and mercy because he does not point to his own experience, his own achievements—vast though the experience is and impressive though his high-risk achievements have been. This is because *his* justice is that of his Lord's, one that Medardo Gómez hears through the Word he must impart, whose way he would embody.

Up front Pastor Gussick forewarns the reader not to expect artful rhetoric. No big deal, he in effect says, about the individual lines and paragraphs of these pages. But he can afford to say this because Bishop Gómez is not unrhetorical; he simply speaks and writes in the unadorned style appropriate to the gospel when it is spoken, heard, and lived in precarious circumstances.

I recall reading the report of an agnostic Jewish newspaper reporter from New York who told of the day when he could empathize with the Christians whose faith could not be his. He had been overhearing Pastor Beyers Naude, a hero of the faith who waged consistent war against the *apartheid* spirit inbred in himself and outspread around him. All Naude did, said the reporter, was to rephrase the biblical story of Naboth and artlessly apply it to the lives of the small, mixed-gender, mixed-race, unimportant congregation that had gathered to hear him.

Those of us who claim to have the faith of Christians know it needs nurture. We take Gussick up on his invitation to listen to this simple, artless, and therefore especially empowering voice of a leader in our time. It might help convert us from the injustice and nonmercy which haunts, tempts, and blights us all—but which need not be the last word about our situation.

Martin E. Marty
The University of Chicago

TRANSLATOR'S PREFACE

The obvious task of a translator is to communicate thoughts that have been expressed in one language through the medium of another. In itself that is no great challenge, provided one is at home in both languages.

However, the art of communication becomes somewhat more difficult if those who read the translation are not "at home" with the environment in which the original thoughts were expressed. It then becomes the obligation of the one interpreting to translate the reader into that other world. That cannot always be done within the text itself. For that reason this preface may help to give background to the homilies that follow.

At first reading, it may seem that Bishop Medardo Gómez has nothing startling to say. The fact is that he is a very soft-spoken man whose style is conversational. When he is in his pulpit, he is always just speaking to the people. There is no show of oratory nor any contrived attempt to draw attention by fancy phraseology or pulpit gimmickry. He speaks simply to his people, many of whom are illiterate or boasting of no more than a second-grade education— the level generally offered in rural schools. But there also are others, well educated and enjoying responsible positions as professionals in their society. All the hearers are there to listen to what this unassuming man in his middle forties has to say.

Perhaps this is best made clear with the following example. If a group of people is sitting in a well-lighted room and someone enters with a flashlight, no one is going to pay much attention. But if that same group is in total darkness, the one with the flashlight will become the focus of attention, because that light is the only source of illumination.

Those of us who come from the middle class of the developed world, growing up with educational opportunities, freedom of religion, and social and economic advantages, are those enjoying the well-lighted environment. But those in El Salvador, like the vast majority of humanity that populates the Third World, have been kept in darkness. Anyone who brings even the faintest glimmer of light into the shadows of their existence will receive their attention. Bishop Gómez is the bearer of light; hence his immense popularity.

Why the darkness in El Salvador and similar world areas? It has to do with history. The light that broke into the Dark Ages of medieval Europe, strangely enough, came from Spain. The prodigious storehouse of ancient Greek learning, kept in the library of Alexandria in Egypt, had been absorbed into the Muslim world. That occurred with the spread of Muslim power after the religious awakening that began with Muhammed in the Arabian desert in the seventh century after Christ. Those Arab Muslims continued westward through north Africa and finally invaded Spain a century later. They established their center of government and learning in Córdova. There Jewish leaders who had escaped to Spain after the Roman conquest of Jerusalem in 70 C.E. and Christians who emigrated earlier to that area sat down with the Muslim savants. For the first, and probably only, time in history leaders of the three religions, Judaism, Christianity, and Islam, shared their wisdom. In this way the treasury of Greek knowledge was translated into Latin and brought into northern Europe by Christian pilgrims who visited the traditional shrine of Saint James in northern Spain.

This new light coming into the darkness of medieval Europe illumined minds and gave impetus to the Renaissance and eventually to the Enlightenment. The ironclad domination of the papacy with the emerging European states was challenged and what followed was called the Reformation in the sixteenth century.

Those two worlds were comprised of medieval Europe with pope and nobility forming the Holy Roman Empire and those who sought

10

the liberation of the soul and mind. Both came face to face in the German city of Worms in 1521 when Martin Luther, representing those who would break with the past, stood before the Holy Roman emperor, Charles V. When Luther refused to recant, with those now famous words, "Here I stand!" he declared that his authority came, not from Rome, but from the Scriptures that the Renaissance had restored to Christendom. Luther claimed the right to interpret the Scriptures by the enlightened and sanctified use of his human reason.

The adolescent emperor, Charles V, was also the king of Spain who at that very moment directed his Spanish armies under Cortés in the conquest of Mexico. This brought Spanish domination to much of the Western Hemisphere, including Central America.

What was developing religiously in northern Europe, in liberating the conscience and granting freedom to study Scripture and reach one's own conviction, never was realized in Spain nor transported to the New World. The Spanish conquerors forced millions of indigenous peoples to accept *their* king and be converted to *their* religion. Without any marked external reform, the Spanish church became the only religion permitted for 300 years.

When freedom from Spain occurred in the 1820s, little changed, for the leaders of independence were, by and large, descendants of Spanish settlers. At the time of the conquest the original lands and their inhabitants were divided and entrusted to the soldiers as reward for their service. The European foreigners controlled the arable lands, forests, mines, and whatever was productive.

Since the middle of the last century, the original Latin Americans attempted to gain control of their own countries. The revolutions had as their root causes the reclaiming of the land and the national patrimony from foreign control.

In Central America the situation was greatly aggravated by the presence of a large indigenous population that exists to this day. This is especially true of El Salvador, since it is the country with the most highly concentrated population in the Americas. But the country's rich agricultural land is owned by a minimal percentage of its citizens. This has forced the landless poor higher into the mountains, where corn and beans must be raised on the least fertile soil.

Religiously, El Salvador's Roman Catholic Church remained most supportive of that economic and political situation. Its bishops were close to the ruling powers, the wealthy families, and a well-armed military. Forty years ago when this writer initiated Lutheran work in Central America, Roman Catholic priests were rarely seen in the rural areas. In 1978 a census was made throughout Latin America, prior to Pope John Paul II's visit to Mexico for the bishops' conference in Puebla. The disproportionate number of priests for the exploding population was shocking. In El Salvador there was only one priest for every 10,000 inhabitants.

The first ray of change in El Salvador flickered in 1930, when the national government promised to begin a land reform program. But it went back on that preelection pledge and called out the army when rural workers demanded justice. In the bloodbath that ensued, an estimated 30,000 landless peasants were massacred. From that day forward the present unrest was unleashed.

In succeeding decades every government failed to bring about reform to meet the demands for land and just working conditions. After Vatican Council II (1965), there was a meeting of the Latin American Roman Catholic bishops in Medellín, Colombia (1968), to discuss the meaning of the council for Latin America. Of special interest was the radical shift that defined the church as "the people of God," not merely the hierarchy to which the laity would be subservient. The new voices favored lay involvement within the Christian community. The forgotten and marginated people gathered in these "base ecclesial communities," as they were called; hence the oft-quoted phrase: the church's "option for the poor."

But not for one moment did this become general policy, nor was it safe to hold out the hand of love and concern to those who had suffered under past economic and social oppression, whose history reached back to the conquest.

The present heated conflict between the Roman Catholic Church and the Salvadoran government stems from the murder of a young Salvadoran priest, Rutilio Grande, in 1977. He had openly supported striking farm workers on a huge sugar plantation. He had preached shortly before the tragic day he was killed, calling the social grievances against the workers a sin. He mocked those among the ruling powers

12

who wanted only a "silent Christ," like those carried in processions, bearing the cross during Holy Week. He boldly declared that soon Bibles coming into El Salvador would be merely the covers, since all the pages, where the prophets and Christ himself spoke against the sins that exploit the poor, the widows, and the orphans, would be declared "subversive" and barred from entry. Shortly after such strong words, while traveling in his car, he was ambushed by machine gunners and killed, together with a child and an elderly man with him.

His close friend, Oscar Arnulfo Romero, who was bishop of the diocese of San Miguel, had just been named archbishop. His election to that highest church office in the country was undoubtedly prompted by his love for books rather than the political arena, and his prior conduct as a team player within the hierarchy. But the murder of his close friend changed all that.

He began to realize what truly was happening in his country. He saw the wholesale injustice. He used his pulpit in the cathedral to speak out against the abuses that were so evident, especially the government's failure to meet the needs of the landless poor and the exploited laborers in the cities. This brought him into open confrontation with the government and the military. He was threatened constantly, but he did not desist.

In his final seven homilies, recorded for history, he spoke, as Jesus had in the temple, pointing his finger at those who abused their power and pleaded with those governing to change. In the final homily he asked the soldiers to stop killing their own people; the last straw had been broken. In a matter of days, while celebrating an evening mass with the sisters at whose hospital he had his humble quarters, he was shot through the heart as he lifted the chalice in the act of consecration. That happened in 1980. No one was ever brought to trial, neither for the murder of Father Grande nor for the murder of Monsignor Romero, who now has become a national martyr.

This was the price paid to bring a flashlight into an unlighted room so that the people could see! In El Salvador the midnight of the middle ages, religiously, economically, socially, and politically, had seen little of the light of the Renaissance, the Reformation, or the Enlightenment that Spain had bequeathed to northern Europe. Spain had never fully adopted for itself these historic antecedents, it never shared them with its colonies in the New World.

Where do the communists and Marxists, mentioned so often during the past decade in the Salvadoran and United States' news media, get into the picture? Where does Bishop Gómez fit into this scenario? After all, together with Roman Catholic, Episcopal, and Baptist fellow Christians, he has been labeled a "communist," a "Marxist," or a "subversive" by some political analysts and even church leaders. How is that possible?

In Europe and eventually in Latin America, wherever the elements in society that wielded economic power ignored the needs of those living off the land or laboring in factories, there were those who spoke out against such abuses. Whenever religious entities in those countries supported such abuses of power and remained deaf to those suffering economic imbalances, there were those who rejected such religions as hypocritical. They became antichurch. One was Karl Marx during the social unrest in central Europe in the 1840s. Marx was of Jewish background, but his parents had become Lutherans—perhaps for political reasons—and their son, Karl, was baptized, confirmed, and married in the Lutheran church.

However, he turned his back on the church he had known in Germany because for him it had no heart for those caught in the economic crush with the industrial revolution. He criticized using capital to create factories and then underpaying the poor peasants who flooded the cities. Karl Marx sided with the social revolutionaries in 1848. When the revolt failed, he sought asylum in England, where, paradoxically, he was supported by his good friend, Friedrich Engels, whose family-owned textile mills were a part of the very system that Marx rejected.

Yet Karl Marx never founded a political party, nor did he instigate any revolutions. His ideology was borrowed by two political movements, both anticapitalist and anticlerical: the communists and socialists. Eventually each became active in the United States and throughout Latin America. Very often they were the workers' only political voices.

14

The Communist party had become active in El Salvador in the early 1930s. They elected mayors in various towns, but the central conservative government never allowed the candidates to be seated. This caused great unrest among the rural and urban poor. In the late 1970s, a national coalition government was appointed in an attempt to satisfy all interests. But the conservative elements would never permit the land reform programs to be implemented. The situation for the landless grew worse.

Finally by 1980 those opposed to the conservative powers withdrew from the coalition government and went underground, initiating armed insurrection. Four liberal political parties, including the communists, began attacking government forces in outlying areas, using the mountains for cover and hiding among the rural poor, who had no alternative but to stay since they had nowhere else to live or grow crops for their families.

The government, branding the rebels "communists," "Marxists," and "subversives," adopted a "burnt earth" policy with United States' military aid in order to flush the rebels from the mountains and destroy their base of sustenance. The rural areas were bombed and machine-gunned from helicopters, driving the people from their homes. In the 1980s, some 60,000 Salvadorans were killed, and 500,000 fled the country and an equal number remained as refugees within their homeland.

This is where Bishop Gómez came into the picture. Early in the 1980s he was president of the Lutheran Synod of El Salvador, pastoring the congregation he had founded in San Salvador. He was greatly frustrated by his ministry. It seemed to him that he was not reaching the people. But with the flood of refugees seeking aid in the capital city, he and his small congregation began to give assistance.

The decisive moment came when the government asked if his congregation would help refugee families who had fled their rural homes on the side of the volcano San Vicente, just east of San Salvador. The Salvadoran Lutherans agreed to give help, but discovered that the demands were well beyond their means. There were 800 individuals involved, mostly women and children with some older men.

At that time Pastor Gómez had received a grant from Norwegian (Lutheran) Church Aid to buy a mobile clinic unit. The money in his hands was just enough to make the down payment on a parcel of land offered by a coffee-grower who was leaving the country. Could he make such a decision and divert the money to meet this humanitarian need? What would be the reaction in Norway? How would the refugees be supported? He took a leap of faith and settled the 800 homeless individuals in the now well-known refugee camp, *Fe y Esperanza* (Faith and Hope).

The Norwegian church agency endorsed his move. Through further grants originating mostly from churches in Europe and the United States, together with local efforts on the part of the refugees, the Salvadoran Lutheran church under Gómez's guidance became widely respected for its defense of human rights and the resettling of landless refugees in El Salvador, either on newly procured land or back in their home areas. All this was done on a purely human-itarian basis without any political preference.

For this he was accused of collaborating with the "subversives." In the spring of 1984, after leaving the representative of the Nor-wegian church agency at the airport, he and his medical coworker were abducted by a right-wing death squad. Prior to that, such action had always ended in death: that of Rutilio Grande, Oscar Romero, and the four North American women who worked among the rural poor with a Roman Catholic order. But by a miracle, after being held captive for several days—interrogated, tortured, and threatened with death—he was released because of the flood of demands for his safety on the part of Lutheran and other church leaders around the world. His medical coworker remained incarcerated for a longer period, but finally also was freed. The torture he suffered required corrective surgery outside the country, but he is now back working at Gómez's side.

This scrape with death left a lasting impression on Gómez. The fall of that same tragic year, his close friend and fellow pastor, David Fernández of San Miguel, was kidnapped and brutally murdered and mutilated. It was a dark day when Pastor Gómez officiated at his friend's funeral. It had been David Fernández who had brought Medardo Gómez to the Lutheran church in San Miguel where his father was pastor. The two became fast friends at school. Medardo had been a practicing Roman Catholic, confirmed by the then bishop of San Miguel, Oscar Romero. His desire was to enter the priesthood, but instead with his friend, David, he went to the Lutheran seminary in Mexico City.

During that trying decade the Lutheran church in El Salvador voted unanimously to confer on their president the title of bishop. He was elevated to that position of honor on 6 August 1986, at a festive service, held at *Fe y Esperanza*, with 3000 in attendance!

Since that day, in spite of continued threats of death and one period of exile in Guatemala in 1989, after the murder of the six Jesuit priests at the Roman Catholic university in San Salvador, he has remained faithful to his task of living and bringing the gospel to his people. His intensity of conviction was amply substantiated in 1989. The Salvadoran Roman Catholic Church had formally urged the government and opposition leaders to initiate a dialogue to resolve their differences. This was immediately endorsed by the local Lutheran, Episcopal, and Baptist churches. A public manifestation was called to support such efforts toward a peaceful solution. That day the streets of San Salvador were filled with 75,000 people demonstrating for peace! The only bishop to declare publicly his solidarity with the Salvadoran people was Medardo Gómez. That took great courage, because for the first time in recent history the government did not confront a public demonstration with armed force and open fire on helpless victims. Perhaps that personal identification with the popular sentiment launched Bishop G6mez as the moral successor to Oscar Romero.

All Gómez's activity is not dedicated solely to a national cause. His involvement has a definite theological dimension. That becomes apparent in these homilies, understood within their historic setting. They reflect Gómez's understanding of what it means to be a Christian in El Salvador at this crucial hour of its history.

Certain concepts stand out that tie his concerns to Christ's mission and God's plan for his people. It is interesting to note that he speaks more about "love" than about "faith." That may seem strange to those of Lutheran background, accustomed to giving great importance, and rightly so, to the biblical emphasis on *justification by faith,* which became the keystone for Luther's interpretation of Scripture.

Right here there is a great danger for those of us outside of Latin America to assume that the challenge that faced Luther was rather parallel to that existing in Latin America today.

It must be remembered that the way Christianity came to northern Europe one thousand years before Luther defined the kind of Christian environment in which Luther saw God. The road by which Christianity came to Luther's forebears was quite different from the coming of Christianity to Latin America.

The numerous peoples who emigrated from the east and formed the various ethnic and national components of sixteenth century Europe became Christians in a unique way. Their leaders were conquered and drawn into the net of an existing politicized Christian empire, centered in Rome. The new tribal leaders came under Roman control and adopted Christianity as a political gesture that demanded religious unity. Although influenced by a Roman presence and missionary guidance, they never abandoned their linguistic or ethnic differences. That is why Europe today is multilingual and an ethnic salad bowl.

The peoples of these various nations followed their leaders, politically and religiously. They were untouched by the educational advances of those powers that now controlled them. Schooled only in the art of war and the skills of self-preservation that enabled them to emigrate thousands of miles, they eventually were folded into the Christianity of the Mediterranean world like the chocolate spirals in a marble cake. They were part of, but quite distinguishable from, their Mediterranean brothers and sisters.

Their conversion to Christianity retained much that reflected their natural religious beliefs. But of great importance to them was the adjustment from an intellectual belief to a practical faith that could be grasped more by sight and experience. There was a shift from an emphasis on the Trinity—Father, Son, and Holy Spirit, which figured prominently in early Christian attempts to define God—to a focus solely on Christ and the local priest as his counterpart. Christ, as the priests in their natural religions, also assumed an authoritative role. Thus Christ was lifted above human kings and priests, and exercised their power to rule and judge.

With the division of society into the three estates: nobility, clergy, and laity—the latter composed mainly of peasants and serfs—Christ himself stood behind the nobleman and the priest, far above and separate. In keeping with the feudal structure, authority was absolute. The nobleman had the power of life and death over his subjects. In a similar way, the priest, as the only mediator for a God of power, held the keys to heaven or hell for the laity. As a result, Christ was out of direct reach and greatly feared. He could be appeased only through the clergy and the church by penance, pilgrimages or crusades, or indulgences, all of which demanded obedience, sacrifice, or money.

For Luther, Christ was a sovereign king and God of judgment. His fear of the punishment deserved by sin, which he felt unrequited through the church's priestly office, drove him and many others to the monastery to find peace of conscience through a life of perpetual obedience, poverty, and chastity.

But not all who entered the clergy ranks were motivated by pangs of conscience. By Luther's time there was a superabundance of clergy. The feudal system exempted clergy from burdensome taxes, extracted from the poor to sustain the life-style of the nobility, their armies, and the church.

A great lament, expressed openly at that time, complained of the moral laxity and pervading laziness so evident among the clergy. As a result, voices for reform were heard on all sides.

This pressure for change not only exploded with a Luther or a Zwingli against the Roman hierarchy. There were more subtle internal attempts at reform, especially within certain religious orders. Interestingly enough, some of this occurred in Spain at the behest of Queen Isabella of Castile—the patroness of Christopher Columbus.

One branch of the Franciscan order, which sent the first twelve missionaries to Mexico and Central America, came from such a reformed monastery. They were highly motivated men, endued with the homegrown Spanish humanism that echoed the Erasmian idealism—by nature all human beings had free wills and were not to be subjected by others, as the serfs at that time.

Among such exemplary clergy during the conquest were Motolinía, who took an Aztec name to identify with the indigenous people; Sahagún, who wrote the first detailed and sympathetic anthropological study of the religious beliefs and practices of central Mexico; and Bartolomé de las Casas, who fought valiantly against the Spanish abuses of the native population, taking his arguments all the way to Charles V and to the university at Salamanca for his famous debate to combat the current theological premise that the peoples of the Americas were less than human.

These three, with perhaps another dozen, were the exceptions. The lack of priests to serve the conquered tribes created a greatly different situation from that which prevailed in Europe. There was also a completely different methodology in Christianizing the peoples in America. Because they were thought to be inferior, their individual dignity was destroyed by imposing one language, culture, and religion through force. What actually was left, after 300 years of colonial oppression, was a veneer that thinly veiled pre-conquest beliefs, expressed in Christian terminology, but often devoid of Christian substance.

Luther knew a Christ who was a sovereign lord and eternal judge. His fear of Christ drove him into the monastery where he found the Scriptures. In their pages he discovered another Christ. The Christ of the Scriptures was not to be feared, but was the loving, suffering Savior, the mediator between God and his creatures, and the guarantor of life over death.

The human claim on God's promise of forgiveness and life was not dependent on what one *did*, "The one who is righteous will live *by faith*" (Rom. 1:17). That passage unlocked for Luther the eternal truth of God's acceptance of the sinner as forgiven because he trusted Jesus Christ. Such faith was sufficient to quell all fear and make a loving Savior of the hated Christ.

In eastern El Salvador, where Medardo Gómez grew up as a Roman Catholic, what kind of Christ did he know? Out of the religious tortilla that was created from a *masa* of Christian symbols, brought by Spaniards and mixed with natural fears and phobias of a conquered people who were externally Christianized, came a Christ that in Latin America had three guises.

As a baby he was held in the arms of a loving mother, who had been wholly identified with the indigenous Americas as the Virgin of Guadalupe. All other apparitions of the Virgin found on Latin American altars partook of similar attributes. From her, Christ, the helpless infant, received his life, his sustenance, his protection, and his comfort. She was the understanding mother. Even for some, she was still the embodiment of the Mayan-Aztec Earth Mother goddess, so prominent in the pre-conquest religions.

The next image of Christ in Latin America was that of the dying man, emaciated, bloody, hanging helplessly from a cross, and suffering the agonies of death. That Christ was seen on all sides. But the final visage was kept especially for Good Friday, when the dead Christ was venerated, as he lay in his tomb. Within that glass casket he was carried in procession on that most holy Friday of the year, the climax of Latin American Christianity. When the procession entered the church on Good Friday midnight, he lay there for another year. Easter Sunday was no great holiday, for the resurrection was not a vital part of popular religion. By that death, Christ represented a people who were subjugated by the sword and oppressed for centuries and with his people rested from the tragedy of the past.

Young Medardo did not see a Christ whom he feared, but with all Latin Americans he saw a Christ whom he pitied. In that Christ there was no hope. Life was a void because its dignity had been crucified and buried by alien forces.

Far different from Luther, Medardo was not motivated by fear, but by hopelessness. He saw his future in the church as a way to lead his people out of a living death into a future alive with hope. His would be a "theology of life," based upon a resurrected Christ. I have no proof that such was the spiritual metamorphosis of Medardo Gómez. I can only surmise this on the basis of knowing this man of God for many years. I have sensed the inner struggles that have torn at his heart as his Christian faith grew into maturity during those past years of torment and triumph.

But it seems clear to him that the crucial question in Central America today is not whether we are saved by faith alone or through human works that evidence God's grace. In Central America, since over 90 percent of the people have been baptized but never fully evangelized, the essential question to be faced is the *incarnation* of the Christian faith. Saint Paul helps us here: "Do you not know that all of us who have been baptized into Christ Jesus were baptized into his death? Therefore we have been buried with him by baptism into death, so that, just as Christ was raised from the dead by the glory of the Father, so we too might walk in newness of life" (Rom. 6:3-4). Such are to "put on the Lord Jesus Christ" (Rom. 13:14).

Latin American Christianity, as we learned before, ends with the first part of those verses on Good Friday. Easter is hardly celebrated. The evangelization of Latin America must begin with Christ's mission anew. "Jesus came to Galilee, proclaiming the good news of God, and saying, 'The time is fulfilled, and the kingdom of God has come near; repent, and believe in the good news'" (Mark 1:14). The "good news" (the gospel) was that the "kingdom of God" had come at Jesus' appearance for those who repented and believed in the good news. Here "faith" is not merely a confession that distinguishes between two emphases in Christian theology: either the sinner is saved *solely* by faith in Christ's atoning work or is saved as a result of balancing *faith* with *works*. Where faith is placed into such a theological equation, it runs the danger of becoming a mere "formula," a confession, a verbalized description of an orthodox belief.

But in the four gospels, faith is *trust* rather than *belief*. Jesus asked his listeners to trust that he was the bearer of the "good news," that God had kept his promise in sending the Messiah-Savior.

Where such repentance and trust in God's promise are present, there is the "kingdom of God." There, as Saint Paul wrote, is the Easter gospel for all those who are "baptized into his (Jesus') death, . . . so that, just as Christ was raised from the dead . . . we too might walk in newness of life" (Rom. 6:3-4.) The one who trusts is a partaker of Christ's death and resurrection in baptism. This is the resurrected, incarnated life. Within the Christian the Word (Christ) becomes a part of history. The kingdom of God is realized.

That is the Christ preached by Bishop Gómez. The incarnation of Christ in the believer is that the risen Christ bestows upon him life, as Christ himself promised: "I came that they may have life, and have it abundantly" (John 10:10). That is life now and for eternity. That is living in the kingdom of God. What creates the kingdom of God is God's love through Jesus Christ and God's love, made evident in Christian living. Hence, love is emphasized much more than faith. For Gómez *faith* is "trust" born of "love" that has been experienced. Faith is love, reflecting back what was given by God through those who love him. Faith is a matter of the heart, not of the head.

Both faith and love are gifts of the Holy Spirit in the baptized Christian. But for Gómez, as for Saint Paul, the gifts of the Holy Spirit must be given careful attention. At the close of Saint Paul's great chapter on gifts in 1 Corinthians 12, he concludes: "But strive for the *greater gifts*. And I will show you a *still more excellent way*" (1 Cor. 12:31). What follows—the "still more excellent way"—is the great chapter on "love," ending with the well-known verse: "And now faith, hope, and love abide, these three; and the greatest of these is love" (1 Cor. 13:13).

For Gómez also, faith and hope are the "now," and most certainly, those in El Salvador need faith (trust) in a God who keeps his promises daily, that they might have hope for their future within his kingdom. But love will cement all that is temporal with that which is eternal. Love is the temporal and eternal gift of the Holy Spirit. It is to be cherished by the sinner, as the assurance of reconciliation with God for time and eternity, and now shared by the Christian with every other human being. Thus Christ (the Word) becomes incarnated in history.

For Gómez, this love overarches all those within the kingdom. How is the kingdom related to the church? Gómez does not speak of the church, as known in the English-speaking world, as a congregation with a street number and a zip code. That concept is foreign in Latin America, where few identify with a local parish. Even denominations are a new phenomenon, only within recent history. The traditional Roman Catholic Church, brought with the conquest, may have lost its former control of every soul, but it still is seen as the nominal spiritual home of the vast majority.

Gómez sees all Christians, all who have come together around Christ, as the kingdom of God in that place. Here is the kingdom; here is the church. "Where two or three are gathered in my name,

I [Christ] am there among them" (Matt. 18:20). Christ is with his people. He is incarnate in his people. The Word (Christ) is within their history. This is the human and divine dimension of the gospel presence. Wherever his people are found, Christ is at work. He becomes a part of their history.

They are his ecumenical presence. Often I have purposely not translated the word "ecumenical" into English, but rather used the original concept of "world-embracing." In our context, ecumenical most often means the coming together of the leaders of Christian denominations or the joint celebration of a service by two or more congregations of different backgrounds. This is not the sense in Gómez's appreciation of the term. For him it is the kingdom of God wherever Christians are together. When Christians in El Salvador face the same enemies who wish to silence their witness, they come together in solidarity to find strength in Christ and in each other. God's love binds them together creating a mutual love that embraces the world.

I close with an image that has never been erased from my memory. At one of my first visits to El Salvador in the late 1940s, early on a Sunday morning with the streets empty, I saw a woman, doubled over in pain, seated on the edge of a curb, her feet stretched out in the gutter. She looked eighty, but perhaps she was closer to forty. She was filthy; her clothes ragged. She was moaning from intestinal distress and uncontrollable diarrhea.

Today a Bishop Gómez would approach such a human being, one suffering undignified agony—the result of a society that dehumanizes people—and speak to her in her own idiom. Perhaps she would not be impressed by him, because she probably has been deceived by sweet words, especially from men, many times before. He would not talk to her, but see that someone from his parish would bring the woman to where her bodily infirmities could be treated. Others out of love would assist her to find that dignity God had given her. She would be reintegrated into her world, perhaps even into her family. I can imagine her face today among those hundreds who crowd the Lutheran Church of the Resurrection every Sunday morning to join with fellow Christians to find a loving and forgiving God in Jesus Christ and a resurrected life with the Holy Spirit. There she, too, would be incorporated into the body of Christ, as part of the kingdom. In her, also, the Word, Jesus Christ, would become her history.

Robert F. Gussick
Day of Saint James

INTRODUCTION:

MEDARDO ERNESTO GÓMEZ

A MAN OF DESTINY

W hen Bishop Medardo Ernesto Gómez asked me to write a few
words as an introduction to this first volume of his homilies, now
to be published under the title, *And the Word Became History,* in truth,
I felt honored and humbled at the same time. I am not a Salvadoran
nor a Latin American. Yes, I have been involved almost fifty years
with the Spanish-speaking world, including twenty-five years when
I lived and worked in Central America. Yet from my point of view,
the foreigner, as missionary, is nothing more than a helper or an
apprentice, offering support to the people among whom he or she
lives and serves in order to extend the kingdom of God. For that
reason, it is an inestimable honor to be considered worthy to intro-
duce the readers to what follows.

Medardo Ernesto Gómez is a man of destiny. This is not in the
sense of the fatalist who chants the ditty: *"¡Que será, será!"* (What
will be, will be!), but in harmony with what Saint Paul exclaimed:
"We know that all things work together for good for those who love
God, who are called according to his purpose" (Rom. 8:28).

For don Medardo[1] God had his purpose. Medardo Gómez has
been recognized for his efforts on behalf of human rights and his

---

1. The term *don,* as used in many parts of Latin America, is an antiquated
Spanish title of respect, from the Latin word, *dominus* (lord).

demands for justice as a Christian expression for the dignity of every human being. He is either applauded or hated because of his insistence on procuring peace by urging dialogue between the opposing sides of the civil war in El Salvador. But how many know about the Christian undergirdings that support that for which he struggles?

I have known don Medardo for many years. Directly or indirectly I remember him since his days in the seminary in Mexico City and afterward as a pastor in Gualán, Guatemala, not far from Zacapa, where my wife and I initiated Lutheran work in Central America in 1947, and now during the last two decades in San Salvador. In August 1986, at the express wish of Salvadoran Lutherans, he was honored with the title of Bishop of the Lutheran Church of El Salvador, of which he was then president. I participated in that historic moment.

His way of dealing with people has not changed through the years. It has been always the same: frank, honest, understanding, loving, and, above all, evangelical. With regard to his ministry he has gone through a radical change. But in his life, his gospel-oriented conduct has not been diminished. More than anything else, this gospel emphasis has opened another dimension, another vision, enabling him to communicate the good news of Jesus Christ.

Having served on various occasions as don Medardo's interpreter when he was in the United States, I remember one of his accounts as to how his understanding of his role as pastor changed. Upon leaving the seminary to serve the congregation in Gualán and afterward in San Salvador, don Medardo felt very frustrated. He felt that what he had learned in the seminary about taking the gospel to people was useless. Was the gospel only communicated with words? There was no shortage of words in Central America with the competition of numberless sects. Their message was, very often, nothing more than endless wordy arguments about Bible interpretations.

Ten years ago with the intensifying of the civil war in El Salvador, being a pastor conscientious about his spiritual responsibility, don Medardo began to read the four Gospels with new insight. There he discovered something: another kind of ministry. It was the ministry of Jesus himself, which did not consist solely in a presentation of the gospel through words, but a gospel incarnate. The life of Jesus was the gospel lived in the midst of the people. Jesus always was active

28

as a servant, surrounded by people. He was looking for them; he was not just waiting for them to find him. Day after day he was in the midst of the most needy, answering the pleas of the sick, the lepers, the paralytics, the deaf, the dumb, and the widows. In that way the multitudes could appreciate him, truly, as the Son of God.

With that new vision of ministry, don Medardo was converted into another kind of servant-minister. From then on he was intimately involved with the victims of his country's civil war. He went to seek them, together with the faithful of his congregation, and bring them to camps for refugees and displaced people, to clinics for the sick and wounded, to homes for the orphans and to relief centers where food was distributed to the hungry and clothing to the naked. To all of these he went with this witness of Christian love.

Because of that, his concept of evangelism was changed. It was not only to explain the way of life through Bible passages, but it was to live that way of life and imitate what was done by Jesus as recounted in the Bible! For those unable to read, who form the majority of Salvadorans, they saw the gospel lived, not only preached. The sacrifice of Christ and his promise of pardon and of life, confirmed by the resurrection, were experienced with the pastor and his flock, giving meaning, in turn, to the name of the parish in San Salvador, the Lutheran Church of the Resurrection, which Pastor Gómez has served with self-denying dedication since its beginning.

The helpless understood by what was lived, not only by what was preached. Now, everyone knows the story about those countless persons persecuted in El Salvador because they gave testimony to their Christian faith. Among them Lutherans are also found, suffering because of their pastoral concern for the poor, as Jesus prophesied, yet to whom he promised his blessing (Luke 4:16-19; 6:20-26).

David Fernández—son of don Héctor Antonio Fernández, the first Lutheran pastor in San Miguel in eastern El Salvador, where don Medardo was born—became his friend. This whole encounter of Fernández and Gómez was the work of God, since don Héctor Antonio, David's father, was the instrument who brought don Medardo into God's service. Then, eventually, the two friends, David and Medardo, went off together to the seminary. Upon returning home, David followed his father as pastor in San Miguel where he suffered martyrdom for practicing the very same kind of ministry as his lifelong friend. Even before that tragedy, don Medardo had been kidnapped and tortured. But according to God's plan, don Medardo confirmed his promise in that experience: he would remain faithful to the gospel. In that commitment the family was united also: his wife, Abelina Centeno de Gómez and his six children, Balduino, Kenia, Irene, Arisbé, Medardo, Jr., and Bella Esperanza. A family forged in solidarity!

One evening, after having been together the greater part of the day, don Medardo and I returned to the parish of the Resurrection, extremely tired. One of the nurses from the clinic was waiting for the bishop with a critically ill baby. She had been searching un-succesfully the whole afternoon for the medicine prescribed by the doctor. Without a word, don Medardo motioned to the mother and the nurse to climb into the van and we continued looking, going from pharmacy to pharmacy. While we were waiting in the van, I tried to talk with the mother, but she, solely concerned for her sick child, gave no reply, not even a word. Finally, don Medardo and the nurse came out with the medicine. Then, at last, the mother sighed and said to me, "He has saved my child." That is the essence of the ministry of Medardo Gomez: save the suffering, the oppressed, be it the sickness of the body or the suffering within society, both the result of sin. For don Medardo there is a poverty that affects both body and soul. Both must be treated.

One time Medardo Gómez said: "Faith cannot be separated from the questions of the basic necessities of life. That demands a new model of ministry for seeking out the poor within the national re-ality, . . . supporting that model with a theological dimension." I imagine that those sentiments are going to be evident in the pages that follow. May they be a blessing as much for the readers, as they were for those who first heard them!

Robert F. Gussick
The first Lutheran missionary in Central America and the founder of the Lutheran churches in El Salvador and Guatemala.

San Diego, California

1

THE MISSION OF THE CHURCH AS THE PROPHETIC VOICE OF GOD

HOMILY
For the Third Sunday after Epiphany

LESSONS:

Isa. 61:1-6
1 Cor. 12:12-21, 26-27
Luke 4:14-21

Then Jesus, filled with the power of the Spirit, returned to Galilee, and a report about him spread through all the surrounding country. He began to teach in their synagogues and was praised by everyone.

When he came to Nazareth, where he had been brought up, he went to the synagogue on the sabbath day, as was his custom. He stood up to read, and the scroll of the prophet Isaiah was given to

him. He unrolled the scroll and found the place where it was written:
"The Spirit of the Lord is upon
> me,
> because he has anointed me
> > to bring good news to the
> > poor.
> He has sent me to proclaim
> > release to the captives
> and recovery of sight to the
> > blind,
> > to let the oppressed go free,
> to proclaim the year of the
> > Lord's favor."

And he rolled up the scroll, gave it back to the attendant, and sat down. The eyes of all in the synagogue were fixed on him. Then he [Jesus] began to say to them, "Today this scripture has been fulfilled in your hearing" (Luke 4:14-21).

1

THE MISSION OF THE CHURCH AS THE

PROPHETIC VOICE OF GOD

The Beginning of Jesus' Ministry

BROTHERS AND SISTERS: We all remember the circumstances in which Jesus was born. We all have learned that Jesus' birth was by the intervention of the Holy Spirit and Jesus was declared God's Son by God himself. His earthly parents, Joseph and Mary, were like the folk of their day, artisans and laborers, and the couple had other children. Jesus was the oldest and had to work from early on to help support his smaller brothers and sisters, just as it is with us, among our poor families who make up the majority in this country. Very obedient, Jesus remained at home until an adult, until the day came when he himself decided to begin his ministry. Then he left home. We all know how he started his ministry. He chose a group of helpers who accompanied him and helped in the work of spreading the gospel.

He traveled about all the regions bordering Jerusalem. His words were admired everywhere and he became the subject of people's conversation. They asked: "Who is this man? Is he the promised Messiah? Is he one of the prophets?" The whole world, it seemed, expected something from him. His words had divine authority. They had the power to touch human hearts.

At that time there were other well-known orators, but the difference between Jesus and the others was not only that he demonstrated his prowess with excellent discourses, but he did miracles.

He was always working with and helping the needy. He went up and down the byways, and his humility and wisdom impressed the people. As he walked with the people, many gave him offerings that he used to share with the poor in the new areas that he visited.

That was the environment in which Jesus was defining his ministry. His fame grew. Jesus of Nazareth was a household word. This Jesus consoled the afflicted, those broken in spirit. He identified with the poor and announced comfort and hope to the oppressed—those who felt themselves imprisoned and tormented by that great problem that we all share as human beings, our slavery in sin.

His popularity spread because there were many poor people. These humble people followed him. When that happened, his own family, his brothers and sisters, thought that he had become deranged. They complained: "What is happening to our brother as he embarks on this mission and walks the highways and byways?" Probably they also warned him: "Be careful, for they are going to kill you. After all, those whom you helped will abandon you," just as some counsel today. But Jesus had a mission and never lost sight of that purpose.

After many months of preaching throughout various regions of Galilee, he decided to visit the town where he grew up. He went to Nazareth to see his father and mother, as well as his brothers and sisters. While in Nazareth, as was his custom, he went, on the Sabbath or Saturday, to the synagogue, which was like our church. He wished to fulfill his religious obligation by setting aside and dedicating that day to the Lord. In the synagogue, they immediately gave him the book, or scroll, to read the Scripture. At that instant something special happened. It was an epiphany, a manifestation, a revealing of Jesus once again as the Son of God. With this event what the prophet Isaiah had announced in the Old Testament when he foretold the coming of the promised Messiah, the Christ, was confirmed. The evangelist, Luke, describes for us the fusing of this earthly and heavenly moment with great feeling.

His Prophetic Ministry

BROTHERS AND SISTERS: There is a question that we must ask ourselves as Christians: "What is the mission of the Christian church in El Salvador? What is the mission of the Lutheran church in El Salvador?" What I see, brothers and sisters, is that, in a real sense, the Scripture here is also being fulfilled. The church of Jesus Christ, the very living body of Christ, is composed of all of us. We are members of that body that we might be the church, as the prophetic voice of God. Now, more than ever, that church has the protection and guidance of God, because the Holy Spirit is over us.

I suggest that we think for a moment about our people. How does the body of Christ, the church, assert itself in our national context? In truth, the mission of the church today is the same as it was in the world of Jesus Christ. Motivated by the presence of the Holy Spirit within us, the mission of the Lutheran church in El Salvador is announcing exactly what the prophet Isaiah said, and what our Lord Jesus Christ demonstrated with his own exemplary life. It follows that one of our characteristics as part of the body of Christ, as the Lutheran church, is to be a prophetic church, a church that follows the mandate of Jesus Christ who said: "God has commanded me to preach the gospel." What does it mean to announce the gospel, the good news to the poor?

Who are the poor in our land? All of us! Of the five million Salvadorans, more than four and a half million of us are poor. Only a small group, a very reduced number, can consider themselves rich. For us, then, it is good news to know that God is with us.

Let us remember the prophetic word of Isaiah and Jesus' fulfillment: "Yahweh has anointed me to bring good news to the poor, has sent me to heal the brokenhearted." Who are the brokenhearted in our land? All of us! This terrible war has broken our hearts. There are none who can say that they are happy because of this war. If there is one, that person is abnormal and possessed of the devil. I ask those with broken hearts to pray humbly with me to our God: "Help us, Father, because I am brokenhearted. . . ."

Listen to the good news: the Lord has sent us to bring the good news to the poor, to heal the brokenhearted. Let us trust God and put our faith and hope in this word that assures fulfillment, because Christ himself is working in the church that he might become operative within us. The Word of God is a reality. For example, when announcing liberty to the captives, it means that we must assure

35

God's promise to the captives, to those imprisoned, that God is with them and is the hope of their liberation. We also are captives in our liberty, in our apparent liberty. There are so many things that oppress us. We are being alienated by a system that holds us captive: we think more of material things, we exert more effort to satisfy our vanity, and we accept values that are not a part of our culture, those that make us acceptable social beings. What we seek has nothing to do with helping us to live within God's liberty. For that reason we are captives, imprisoned; for that reason we need God's liberating power.

The Church's Mission as the Prophetic Voice of God

Brothers and sisters: I have been blind and only little by little am I beginning to see. Let us examine our lives and let us take note that there is a historic process within which only now do we begin to understand certain contradictions, inner struggles, and conquests. It is essential that God open our eyes wider that we may see with more clarity those aspects of our lives, as individuals, as families, and as a nation, which are not easy to comprehend.

That is the mission of the church, this is the Lord's work throughout all history: to bring good news to the poor, to heal the brokenhearted, to announce liberty to the captives, to give sight to the blind, and to free the oppressed that the year of the Lord's grace become a reality.

Brothers and sisters, this is the great goal of the Christian church. This is the one great challenge that we all have. We know that what Jesus asks of us the world alone can never attain because it lacks the essential: the church. We, as Christ's body, must work with all our efforts and must put on the Spirit of the Lord. We recognize that this all-encompassing message of the prophet Isaiah and the occurrence of its fulfillment, related by Saint Luke, is true. It is something that can happen. There are those of good faith, humanistically motivated, who seek these ends. But this goal, in its widest dimensions, both physical and spiritual, is left for Christians, for the church of Jesus Christ. That goal is left for us, as representatives of a merciful God on earth, in keeping with our Christian faith and life.

From the outset the Holy Spirit must be with us before we even begin to undertake this task before which some may ask us, rather surprisingly: "And you, why do you involve yourself in this kind of work, to help the poor, the oppressed, and the brokenhearted? That is dangerous!" One needs to be vested, as one accepting an office, by the Holy Spirit. That must be the priority of the Christian church from the very beginning: accept the task in a spirit of devotion in order to ask the Lord to inspire us and bless us, because having the Holy Spirit with us, the commitment to proclaim the gospel will be easy. Truly this does not demand effort on our part nor belief in our bravery, since the only valiant one is the Lord. The wisdom in this undertaking is God's. All success will come from him. All we need do is be converted into God's instruments so that the Holy Spirit is with us, in order to fulfill the Scripture through us, as the Christian church, as the Lutheran church of El Salvador. Thus we become the prophetic church, the church that speaks with the voice of God in this time and for this hour. I tell you, brothers and sisters, let us ask God that he send us his Holy Spirit because only by his will can we faithfully fulfill the role of the church of Jesus Christ, the prophetic church that now becomes the incarnate Scriptures for our beloved country of El Salvador. AMEN.

2

THE CHURCH OF JESUS CHRIST MUST PREACH THE TRUTH

HOMILY
For the Fourth Sunday after Epiphany

LESSONS:

Jer. 1:4-10
1 Cor. 12:12-27; 13:13
Luke 4:21-32

Then he began to say to them, "Today this scripture has been fulfilled in your hearing." All spoke well of him and were amazed at the gracious words that came from his mouth. They said,

"Is not this Joseph's son?"

He said to them, "Doubtless you will quote to me this proverb, 'Doctor, cure yourself!' And you will say, 'Do here also in your hometown the things that we have heard you did in Capernaum.'"

39

And he said, "Truly I tell you, no prophet is accepted in the prophet's hometown. But the truth is, there were many widows in Israel in the time of Elijah, when the heaven was shut up three years and six months, and there was a severe famine over all the land; yet Elijah was sent to none of them except to a widow at Zarephath in Sidon. There were also many lepers in Israel in the time of the prophet Elisha, and none of them was cleansed except Naaman the Syrian."

When they heard this, all in the synagogue were filled with rage. They got up, drove him out of the town, and led him to the brow of the hill on which their town was built, so that they might hurl him off the cliff.

But he passed through the midst of them and went on his way.

He went down to Capernaum, a city in Galilee, and was teaching them on the sabbath. They were astounded at his teaching, because he spoke with authority (Luke 4:21-32).

2

THE CHURCH OF JESUS CHRIST MUST

PREACH THE TRUTH

Introduction

BROTHERS AND SISTERS: There is a very human message in today's gospel. It tells us that the children of God understand each other; they come together and unite when faced with pain and suffering. The gospel also points out how the children of evil do not understand the children of God. That is because there is no communion between light and darkness. They are opposites. But the children of evil help each other, even as the children of light are mutually supportive, one toward the other. That is why we, as the Lutheran church of El Salvador, rejoice to welcome from different parts of the world brothers and sisters, children of light, who come here on God's behalf to show their moral and spiritual support. They share with us their Christian love by their understanding, their work, and their meaningful solidarity, just as the gospel tells us.

Jesus Astonished His Townsfolk in Nazareth

Now we are going to study the sacred Scripture for this Sunday and interpret from its Christian insight our moment of history, the situation in which we, as a church, are living. We shall show from the word in today's gospel how God is with us.

But before that, it is interesting to see how our liturgy, because of its own structure and sequence, helps us grow in step with the development and history of Christianity. Recall, for a moment, the gospel of last Sunday, the third after Epiphany, in which Saint Luke spoke to us about the mission of the church, as the prophetic voice of God, through the teachings of Jesus Christ. Last Sunday we saw how the end goal of Christian witness mirrors Jesus' own ministry. In that gospel, Saint Luke tells us the story about Jesus' visit in Nazareth where he was born. There it was, specifically, that Jesus announced that he was to bring the gospel, the good news to the poor.

Today we will see how Jesus came to his hometown to preach. His arrival was preceded by his fame that had extended throughout the regions where he had traveled. When he reached Nazareth, where the people had seen him grow up, where they had seen him playing as a child, where by then his name often was mentioned and he was a celebrity, it was only normal that his townsfolk began to say, when his arrival was imminent: "Jesus has come!" "Which Jesus?" "The son of Mary, you ignoramus. . . ." "But son of which Mary?" "The Mary, wife of Joseph, the carpenter." "He is the one who is coming." "We are going to the synagogue, to the church, because probably he will be there too. . . ."

The church was full. Everyone wanted to hear Jesus. In the synagogue were the important people as well as the humble folk of the village, all waiting to hear what he would tell them.

As was custom, they handed the visitor a scroll of the Scriptures, that of Isaiah. Upon reading the specified verses Jesus revealed to them that those sacred words were fulfilled in him at that moment. With that as introduction, he left them astonished. He was an eloquent and wise man. All listened attentively to what Jesus said. The gospel says that they were all astonished, even uplifted by his words; they were truly impressed by this Jesus. Yet, among them, some grumbled: "Well and good! Isn't this the son of Joseph, the carpenter? Isn't he the son of Mary? Where does he get all that knowledge?" Others, undoubtedly, admired him and even felt somewhat proud to be his friend. In him they saw someone who was from their own village and who now had gained prestige in other places, in other communities where he had preached and carried out his work through the Holy Spirit. There he was standing before them, in his own village of Nazareth, the same Jesus, consecrating himself as the Son of God.

Jesus Reveals the People's Sins

Today's gospel describes for us how things began to change the moment Jesus preached in the synagogue to those in his hometown. After the Lord's beautiful introduction about which all marveled and after his eloquent exposition that demonstrated his insight, he began to point out the sin and injustice in which they were living. He told them that they were denying God and because of the lack of faith, God had not been evident among them. It was necessary that they regain their faith to experience the presence of the Holy Spirit in their lives.

Then their attitude began to vacillate. Those individuals who in the beginning showed such admiration for Jesus began to feel offended and became angry because he was pointing out their sin. But so it is, brothers and sisters, the church of Jesus Christ has to preach the truth. It has to denounce injustice, come what may. It has to point out sin and the sinner, whoever he or she may be. But people do not like that. As a result, they began to despise Jesus.

Facing this negative reaction on the part of his townsfolk, Jesus cited some very pointed examples. "Look," he said, "God is not evident in your midst, because some of you are unbelievers and live unrighteous lives. You better look at Scripture and what it says about that widow in Zarephath, who for her goodness knew God's presence, giving her protection, even providing her with food in her necessity and allowing her to share with the prophet in her home to help him with his needs. The same thing happened with Naaman, the Syrian, who for his goodness experienced the presence of God. That is the way you should be. Live justly and believe, keeping faith in God, that God might make himself known to you."

They became so angry that they grabbed him and took him to the top of the mountain on which their town was built. From there they wanted to throw him down.

Some Want to Destroy the Church Today

What they did to Jesus, that is what the sons of evil wish to do with the Christian church in our time, with our testimony enmeshed in history. They want to destroy the church of Jesus Christ, because they cannot bear to confront that which denounces injustice and tells the truth. The children of darkness want something completely different. They want a church that is docile and distant. Here, brothers and sisters, let us pay careful attention. Let us not be confused. Some have called the devil "Luzbel," which means "beautiful light," giving an appearance that is pleasing and translucent. Let us be very careful of those private gatherings of so-called Christians, where it seems that God is resplendent in brilliant light, because in that atmosphere there are no problems, no suffering or persecutions, and everything is said to go well, even giving the false impression that what appears is a divine revelation and produces an emotional high. Be careful brothers and sisters. "Luzbel" deceives. "Luzbel" assumes the appearance of the truth.

Our Church and the Divine Truth

When everything appears so appealing, when situations are described as being free of any problem, just like the temptation of Adam and Eve, insinuating that they were misinformed, then especially let us be careful. When someone wishes to insist that here we can make our mark, because this is what we are seeking, be wary of this "beautiful light" as an answer to our doubts and as a recipe to make us feel better and more fulfilled.

Brothers and sisters, let us be especially careful, for according to the signs indicating the fate of the church of Jesus Christ, it is apparent that as they took our Lord to that place to throw him down, in like manner there are those who would destroy the Christian church today.

But those of us who understand the message that God's Word brings us, we already know that Christ was crucified. Christ conquered death and sin. Never again can they destroy him, nor can they do him any harm. The work of God our Father cannot be detained, because Christ, his Son, has already triumphed; he is risen! God, as he helped his Son, assuring him while he walked safely through the midst of those threatening to kill him, that he could leave them without harm, gives us the same promise of divine protection that is constant and eternal. God will remain with us. He raises our spirits and counsels us, saying: "Do not be afraid, because I am and will remain with you, always until the end of the world."

Brothers and sisters, I know that as a result of the misinterpretations about our pastoral and social work and the threats and attacks against our church, many of us are afraid. I can only say to you, that Jesus, being the Son of God, identified with the poor, having become a human being, was also afraid at times, as now, when they wished to throw him off the mountain. For that very reason, Jesus Christ and God, our Father, will not let us be deceived when "Luzbel" suggests: "Better come over here with us, for here there will be no problems, no persecutions, and everything will go well."

Be careful, brothers and sisters, when deeds and doers who represent the forces of evil recommend, tempting us, that we abandon the cause of the kingdom of God.

I have had that temptation. I confess, being the weak person that I am. It came to me as a voice, counseling that I abandon that concept that I hold of Christ as a human and divine being within a real society. I have felt that temptation when I have put my life before the souls of others; when I have valued my own safety more than yours, my beloved ones in Christ.

A Pastoral Interpretation of the Gospel

As human as I am, I have repeatedly mentioned my weaknesses. But I also can affirm the confession of my faith in the gospel. With my experience as pastor within the historic situation of our church, I can say with an unabashed Christian determination that God is present. I see a people in its entirety when all of you reveal yourselves to me as the body of Christ in our nation. You give me your confidence, you uphold me, you perceive me to be your spiritual guide during our present social and historic conditions.

45

God manifests himself when the entire international community expresses to our church, in concrete fashion, its confidence, its support, comprehension, and solidarity.

That is how I feel and together all of us sense that the Lord is revealing himself to us. For that reason before our Father and Jesus Christ we commit ourselves with greater fervor to remain faithful to God, with the surety that the evil is never going to destroy us as a church, because God is protecting us as he inspires us and urges us to fulfill with our lives his sacred gospel. AMEN.

May the peace of God that surpasses all understanding strengthen us and keep us in the true faith.

3

THE CHURCH OF JESUS CHRIST WILL RECEIVE ETERNAL GLORY

HOMILY
For the Last Sunday after Epiphany

LESSONS:

Deut. 34:1-12
2 Cor. 4:3-6
Luke 9:28-36

Now about eight days after these sayings Jesus took with him Peter and John and James, and went up on the mountain to pray. And while he was praying, the appearance of his face changed, and his clothes became dazzling white. Suddenly they saw two men, Moses and Elijah, talking to him. They appeared in glory and were speaking of his departure, which he was about to accomplish at

47

Jerusalem. Now Peter and his companions were weighed down with sleep; but since they had stayed awake, they saw his glory and the two men who stood with him. Just as they were leaving him, Peter said to Jesus, "Master, it is good for us to be here; let us make three dwellings, one for you, one for Moses, and one for Elijah"—not knowing what he said. While he was saying this, a cloud came and overshadowed them; and they were terrified as they entered the cloud. Then from the cloud came a voice that said, "This is my Son, my Chosen; listen to him!"

When the voice had spoken, Jesus was found alone. And they kept silent and in those days told no one any of the things they had seen (Luke 9:28-36).

3

THE CHURCH OF JESUS CHRIST
WILL RECEIVE ETERNAL GLORY

Introduction

Bᴿᴏᴛʜᴇʀꜱ ᴀɴᴅ ꜱɪꜱᴛᴇʀꜱ: The context in which the transfiguration
of Jesus takes place is as follows: Jesus was very concerned and fear
welled up constantly within him. The conflict grew out of the tension
created by his becoming, as the Son of God, also a true human with
flesh and blood that he might carry out the will of his Father, our
God, who chose that he not be born as the son of a king, but of
humble people, artisans and laborers. In that way he could identify
with the conditions of the poor and feel a solidarity with those who
at that time were practically slaves. Within that world, as his ultimate
purpose, he was to demonstrate a profound love for all humanity
throughout the entire world. In that simple, yet complex role of
being truly human, he felt fear, mostly when he announced and
proclaimed the kingdom of God in the towns and villages. For by
dedicating himself to bring the "good news to the poor," to "announce liberty to the prisoners," and to say that he came to "give
freedom to the oppressed," his words and his cause were misinter-
preted and at the same time clashed with the local political powers
and the empire itself.

Jesus knew exactly what his situation was if he were to remain
faithful to his divine mission. He did not ignore the fact that because
of his eloquence and wisdom, and especially his deeds, he was greatly

admired and people followed him wherever he went preaching. But he also knew that those who were loyal to him, the people of God, would suffer persecution. Believers would be thrown into jail and killed for following his way, his truth, and his life, all that he, as Jesus Christ our Lord, taught by his example. Jesus foresaw the future of his apostles, as well as the saints, servants, and believers. He knew that many would die as martyrs, even as he. His cross was not only weighted by his own suffering, but it carried the pain and the worry for the others, for all those faithful to the gospel. Because of this, Jesus was burdened by a deep sadness; he saw fear in the faces of many of his followers. This caused him anxiety to the degree that at times he wondered if perhaps the way he had taken was the correct one. Jesus was facing a crisis: he had to know if the way he had chosen was the path of truth. He had to be assured, humanly speaking, if in reality he were the Son of God.

Jesus Was Confirmed as the Son of God by His Apostles

Jesus by his practice taught us how to meditate, reflect, and pray in moments of crisis. He exemplified this positive way to find spiritual help. In the face of uncertainties about his role in the world, Jesus followed a devotional practice together with his apostles. They made such a retreat in Caesarea Philippi, where the Master asked his disciples: "Who did they think Jesus was?" "Who really was he?" There he also asked them: "Who do the people say that I am?" "Who do the people say is the Son of Man?"

To that they answered: "Some say that you are John the Baptist; others, one of the prophets of old who has been resurrected." After those answers, Jesus turned and asked them: "If that is who the people say that I am, who do you say that I am?" With that Peter answered: "Lord, you are Christ, the Son of the living God."

At that moment, with the response of Peter, I imagine that Jesus was very happy, because from his disciples he received spiritual confirmation and consolation: they affirmed that he was the Son of God, they truly recognized him as the promised Messiah. With that Jesus was filled with profound satisfaction. He could feel content because his disciples confessed him to be the Lord, the Son of God, the Messiah promised by the prophets, the one humanity awaited.

Receiving that confirmation from the apostles, Jesus began to explain to them that if they recognized him to be the Son of God, they must also know from Scripture that he had to go to Jerusalem. At that moment Jesus was truly conscious of what Scripture had said, centuries before his birth, about his eventual death. Now he had to pass those tests to prove his sonship with God, as the incarnate chosen one, by a faithful fulfillment in both his life and his death that the church might become his eternal witness.

With that announcement of death, Peter intervened, took Jesus aside, and reproached him: "Do not go to Jerusalem; because if you do, they are going to kill you! . . . Jerusalem is known for its martyring of prophets!"

In spite of this best of intentions by Peter, Jesus became angry and said: "Get away from me, Satan! because you do not understand the things of God. You are only concerned about the things of this world."

Jesus Confirmed by the Law and the Prophets

Eight days after this conversation, according to Saint Luke, Jesus decided to put the question about who he was directly to God, since he now knew what the people thought and what his disciples believed about him. Now he wanted God to confirm who he was. Together with Peter, James, and John, he climbed a very high mountain. It is thought that it was Mount Hermon, which is close to Jerusalem. There he wished to commune with God to ascertain who he really was, if he was on the right way, and if he should go to Jerusalem. There, according to today's gospel, Jesus began to pray, directing himself to his Father and asking him: "Father, am I really your Son? Father, is it certain that I must go to Jerusalem or have I chosen the wrong path? Is this the real way out, that foreordained exodus, that pilgrimage and journey that I must make?" While he was praying a dazzling light shown on him, his face took on a different aspect, and his clothing became brilliantly white. In the midst of that resplendent light, two persons appeared. One was Elijah and the other, Moses.

51

The evangelist says that the three shone with a bright light, surrounded by an aura of glory, while speaking about Jesus' departure (exodus) for Jerusalem and the mission that he had to complete there.

There with Jesus were two representatives from the Old Testament, Elijah, the greatest of the prophets, and Moses, the greatest of the lawgivers. This event was telling Jesus that the law and prophecy of the old covenant approved the course that Jesus had chosen according to God's direction. It was right that he go to Jerusalem, that thus history was being confirmed. Elijah and Moses were assuring Jesus that implicit in God's plan of salvation for his creation was that Jesus go to Jerusalem.

Jesus Confirmed by God, as His Son, His Chosen One

There on that mountain those witnesses had affected an epiphany, which means a manifestation, an apparition, a divine revelation. We saw how Jesus received the approval of history from the old covenant's laws and prophecy. Elijah and Moses told him that he was on the right way, Jerusalem bound. Jesus, who knew only too well the social and political turmoil of his times, knew that to complete his prophetic mission he had to suffer much. He would be rejected, branded and persecuted, imprisoned, tortured, and then crucified by the Jewish and Roman authorities, and at the hands of both the priestly aristocracy and the masters of the law. To go to Jerusalem meant, then, to choose the cross. His anxiety still loomed large and he needed an even greater confirmation of his course of action, if it was indeed the correct one with God's approval. With such thoughts still seeking resolution in Jesus' mind, a cloud enveloped him, together with James, Peter, and John, who had accompanied him during this time alone for reflection and meditation in prayer. That cloud represented the glory of the Father, the glory of God. In all the history of the children of Israel, whenever a cloud appeared, it indicated the presence and protection of God. Out of the cloud, which enveloped Jesus and the three apostles, there came a voice that said: "This is my beloved Son. Listen to him!"

52

As the Church We Shall Follow God's Guidance

BROTHERS AND SISTERS: Our country is in the midst of convulsive events and in this context our church has to live. As Christians, we share great anxieties: the violence that torments our country and our option for peace, the path that, as a church, we have chosen.

Last night, as I was meditating, I thought of how, as a church and as the body of Christ, it is fitting that we ask the Lord if we are on the right way. We should ask the Lord if we must go to Jerusalem, which signifies sacrifice. Jerusalem is a synonym for problems. That is why Peter said to Jesus: "Do not go to Jerusalem!" To that Jesus replied: "Get away from me, Satan! because you do not know the things of God; your sight is fixed only on what is human!"

Thinking about all of that, brothers and sisters, we must pray, as did our Lord Jesus Christ. In his devotional life, he experienced a manifestation of God. His heavenly Father made himself apparent in Jesus' devotional life, especially when he was praying. In the same way, as long as our church follows a devotional discipline, we, as its children, will hear the voice which says to us: "Jesus is the Son of God. We are to hear him!" For that reason, in my commitment to you, as your pastor, I can assure you, my brothers and sisters, that we are only going to follow the way in which God directs us, the path that God indicates. We are not going to travel in other directions. We are only going to take as our map the Word of God, which has taught us for twenty years that Jesus Christ is the beloved Son of God, his chosen one.

Brothers and sisters, let us concentrate our energies, as a church, on completing our prophetic mission in our country, as it has been commended to us. But we must also apply this way of living in our homes, in our lives together, and in our personal walk. Jesus Christ is the Son of God. Only to him will we give our obedient attention, and the glory of God will be manifested to us to guide our church correctly, as well as our homes and the lives of each one of us. AMEN.

4

JESUS CHRIST IS THE CONQUEROR OF ALL TEMPTATIONS

HOMILY
For the First Sunday in Lent

LESSONS:

Deut. 26:5-10
Rom. 10:8b-13
Luke 4:1-13

Jesus, full of the Holy Spirit, returned from the Jordan and was led by the Spirit in the wilderness, where for forty days he was tempted by the devil. He ate nothing at all during those days, and when they were over, he was famished.

The devil said to him,

"If you are the Son of God, command this stone to become a loaf of bread."

Jesus answered him, "It is written, 'One does not live by bread alone.' "

Then the devil led him up and showed him in an instant all the kingdoms of the world. And the devil said to him,

"To you I will give their glory and all this authority; for it has been given over to me, and I give it to anyone I please. If you, then, will worship me, it will all be yours."

Jesus answered him,

"It is written, 'Worship the Lord your God, and serve only him.' "

Then the devil took him to Jerusalem, and placed him on the pinnacle of the temple, saying to him,

"If you are the Son of God, throw yourself down from here, for it is written,

'He will command his angels concerning you, to protect you,' and 'On their hands they will bear you up, so that you will not dash your foot against a stone.' "

Jesus answered him,

"It is said, 'Do not put the Lord your God to the test.' "

When the devil had finished every test, he departed from him until an opportune time (Luke 4:1-13).

4

JESUS CHRIST IS THE CONQUEROR

OF ALL TEMPTATIONS

Introduction

Brothers and sisters: The season of Lent has started, which in simple terms means a period of forty days. However, for us Christians this season is filled with much biblical and religious significance of great importance, since Lent gathers together the great historic traditions that reveal to us God's plan of salvation.

In various parts of the Bible, as much in the Old Testament as in the New Testament books that deal with Jesus Christ and his gospel, we find references to the happenings remembered during this forty-day period set aside for Lent.

It is interesting to note how frequently the number "forty" appears in relation with other biblical occurrences, so that it assumes a symbolic meaning in the Scripture.

This expression of forty years or forty days, repeated again and again in the Bible, is elevated to a symbolic significance, a sacred key word, full of history, faith, and the hopes of all the believers in the world.

The promise of salvation through our Lord is given to all of God's people in all the earth, because as much in the beginning of the Bible narrative as in the time of the New Testament, the period of forty days signifies a tremendous test of faith, a divine revelation, an act of consecration, or the triumph of the children of God against the evil of temptation.

That is what happened during the universal flood when it rained over all the face of the earth for forty days and forty nights. The pilgrim people of God wandered in the wilderness for forty years. Moses was on Mount Sinai for forty days. The prophet Elijah fled from the vengeance of perverse Queen Jezebel for forty days and forty nights, because in her zealous worship of Baal she had killed all the other true prophets of the Lord.

The Forty Days of Jesus Christ

In a similar way this sacred sign of forty days and forty nights is found in the New Testament. This religious code number, which was apparent in the history of Jesus' ancestors, again returns in the life of the beloved Son of God, our Lord Jesus Christ.

This time it is the forty days that Jesus Christ was fasting in the desert, where he was tempted and tested until he conquered the devil.

For that reason we Christians give the name "Lent" (in Spanish it is *cuaresma,* related to the word *cuarenta,* which means "forty") to this period of forty days in which we prepare ourselves for Easter. It begins with Ash Wednesday and ends with Jesus' passion, death, and resurrection, celebrated especially during what we know as Holy Week.

It is very important to meditate on today's gospel when beginning Lent. It offers a goal, a challenge to prepare all of us to celebrate the true significance of Holy Week.

The Temptations of Jesus for Us in Our Time

The gospel for today relates for us the temptations that Jesus suffered in the desert.

We are going to examine, one by one, these temptations that the devil devised to test our Lord. We will see how at this very moment of our history that same voice manifests itself and tempts us to sin.

Here we will learn, according to Christian teaching, what a temptation really is and what different forms it may take. We also want to learn how we can fight and conquer temptations with the Spirit of our Lord.

All of us, as human beings, are tempted where we are weakest. Those who believe in God as well as those who reject him are tempted.

But the temptation of one who does not believe is distinct from that which comes to the believer.

I would say that for those who do not believe in God a temptation may be defined as nothing more than a permanent persuasion to do wrong. It is seductive, inviting one to commit sin. It attempts to convince a person to choose the wrong way. To persuade, to seduce to go wrong is basically what temptation means for the nonbeliever.

For the believer, temptation means much more than that. Certainly believers also experience that which persuades and seduces to sin, but it is more than just defending against evil insinuations. Temptation for Christians means being *put to the test*, as today's gospel teaches.

Put to the Test According to the Bible

Various stories in the Bible tell us about servants of God, his children, who although wholly dedicated to him, were tempted and put to the test.

Do you remember the story of Job? He was tested at the precise moment in his life when he enjoyed the greatest prosperity. He had untold possessions and enough children to help him reap his harvests and make good profits. In spite of his riches, Job loved God and averted evil, treating his laborers well and living a devout life with his family.

But the moment came when God permitted the devil to tempt Job. In that way God wanted to demonstrate that when someone was truly faithful to him, no matter how strong the temptations, that person would not fall away.

That temptation Job passed through was a terrible test: all his children died; he lost all his possessions; his whole body suffered an unbearable illness. He endured sores with scabs all over his body.

The pain sapped all his physical and emotional strength, and the scabs drove him to despair. Finally he could not bear to wear clothing and just sat naked on the ground. After that his wife abandoned him. Then his friends came and instead of comforting him they only tormented him more. After they abandoned him, he remained faithful to God, praying fervently:

> Naked I came from my mother's womb,
> and naked shall I return there;
> the Lord gave, and the Lord has taken away;
> blessed be the name of the Lord. (Job 1:21)

The First Temptation: The Temptation Within Society

What follows is a sign for the people of God, for the church of Jesus Christ, and for all of us, as church, to learn about temptation. In the New Testament our Lord Jesus Christ himself teaches us. He tells about how his first temptation came about, in these words:

> [Jesus] was led by the Spirit [of God] in the wilderness, where for forty days he was tempted [put to the test] by the devil.
> He ate nothing at all during those days, and when they were over, he was famished.
> The devil then said to him,
> "If you are the Son of God, command this stone to become a loaf of bread."
> Jesus answered him, "[The scripture says], 'One does not live by bread alone.' "

This temptation, beloved brothers and sisters, is the kind of temptation that we suffer within society. It is physiological. It is the temptation that deals with all of our necessities for life. It is the temptation to rob, to injure, and to kill for a price. This is the temptation that comes to us many times, trying to convince us, with evil intent, to do this or that. It is inviting and deceiving, all the while assuring us: "No one is going to take notice. Do it! Rob! Kill! Injure! No one will see you!" That is the way Satan operates! That is the way in which temptation dresses itself in our society.

60

Right now in our country, where there is a high percentage of unemployment with no job opportunities, we are often tempted to rob. Many times the same devil is dressed as a friend, like someone close to us, who invites us to sin: "Come on, do that! Go ahead, don't be a fool! Let's do it! No one is going to see anything. We can get something we need, we can lay our hands on a lot of money and in that way change our present situation!"

Jesus also suffered this temptation, just like all the temptations that come to us in our lives. They tempt us to obtain more of this world's goods like money, good clothes, pleasures, and luxuries so that our lives might be better. Such persuasion on the part of Satan is used to seduce us because of our love for money, for the power of riches, or other material advantages.

Brothers and sisters, the Scripture teaches us how to respond with the Spirit of the Lord in our hearts, face to face with such seduction, which is merely a disguise for Satan. The Scripture says: "One does not live by bread alone." And it adds: "But strive first for the kingdom of God and his righteousness, and all these things will be given to you as well" (Matt. 6:33).

Having God in these difficult times of testing, we will always receive his help. He will give us bread. He will help us in the struggles, as we trust in his divine presence and strive to earn our bread.

But what he does not wish is that we stoop to kill, to rob, to hurt, simply to amass money. For that reason the great teachers of the Christian faith speak to us about what are "the true riches" (1 Tim. 6). They tell us why people kill, rob, and hurt others. People are driven by selfishness at the expense of their souls. "For the love of money is a root of all kinds of evil, and in their eagerness to be rich some have wandered away from the faith and pierced themselves with many pains" (1 Tim. 6:10).

The Second Test: The Political Temptation

The evangelist Luke tells us how the devil continued to tempt Jesus during those forty days, after the first fiasco.

This time "the devil led him up and showed him in an instant all the kingdoms of the world. And the devil said to him, 'To you I will give their glory and all this authority; for it has been given over to me, and I give it to anyone I please. If you, then, will worship me, it will all be yours.' "

But Jesus replied: "It is written, 'Worship the Lord your God, and serve only him.' "

This temptation, my beloved, is a political temptation. To the church also these opportunities are offered. On two occasions, for example, I found myself, as a representative of the church, with people who told me: "Tell us how much money you need to carry out your work. All that you need will be given you. Just tell us! You don't have to be limited by lack of resources! Do you want to build a cathedral? We can help you build a cathedral! It is not necessary to suffer privation and other problems in your pastoral work and social ministry. You can have power! How much money do you need?"

Within the church, too, we must be careful about those who make enticing offers that hinge on temptations, because underneath the offers there are hidden intentions that spell evil. We must realize that when they take the church to the top of the mountain, to the apex of power, it is there that Satan repeats to us also: "Look, all that riches I offer you: the glory, the power of the whole world I will give you, if in exchange you worship me!"

If the church were to succumb to that temptation, it would mean no longer preaching the gospel from our perspective as a prophetic and historic church, according to our concept of the Christian faith by which we have opted to help the poor in our ministry.

The Temptations of Power

BROTHERS AND SISTERS: That temptation of power also comes to each of us. Many times to rise to a certain position in our jobs or make our mark in whatever humane or social endeavor we may be, we want power, we want to be important, we want to dominate others, we want to be recognized because of our authority and control.

There are those who have no qualms even as they invent slanderous and rash stories, nor does it cause them any remorse to defame or destroy the good name of another. It means nothing to them to fire others, because their sole interest is to stay on top, without thinking for a moment how they hurt individuals and families.

Those are actual temptations that we observe daily. Tragically, that kind of alienating social behavior receives applause in our Salvadoran society. Selfishness, which grows out of a lack of love for the neighbor, is the source for much bad behavior, like intrigue, opportunism, bootlicking, blackmail, disloyalty, and thirst for power that results in losing the faith and failing to appreciate human endeavors.

Those are the temptations that we face daily in our country. For that reason, my brothers and sisters, God calls us to be the church, a congregation, a group of Christians. God calls me, as a representative of the church. All of us, who are his children, each one of us, believers and nonbelievers, are put on the alert with that temptation.

Great importance must be given then to the test that seduces to obtain large amounts of personal possessions, big bank accounts, commodious comfort, and immeasurable power.

The Third Test: The Spiritual Temptation

After the devil had failed in tempting the Lord about everyday needs for physical life or in fanning his human appetite for knowledge and power, he devised a much more subtle strategy, more dangerous, against Jesus Christ.

The devil had seen the power of our Lord, who even when he was dying of hunger in the desert did not yield to the temptation of selling his soul for a loaf of bread by betraying his God.

Nor did Jesus Christ succumb when faced with the diabolic offer of great earthly possessions, power, riches, and dominion over the nations of the world in exchange for surrendering his spirit of love, peace, and justice by worshiping and serving the devil.

The devil had to invent, then, a very smart strategy, piercingly potent in its maliciousness. He conspired to engage Jesus Christ in a battle of ideology and theology. He approached that weak side we all possess: our vanity, our assurance about our own importance that we are the epitome, the chosen ones, tops in knowing our specialties. In this temptation he attacked Jesus' spiritual ego.

Today's gospel tells us that "the devil took him to Jerusalem, and placed him on the pinnacle of the temple, saying to him, 'If you are the Son of God, throw yourself down from here, for it is written, "He will command his angels concerning you, to protect you," and "On their hands they will bear you up, so that you will not dash your foot against a stone." ' "

"Jesus answered him,

" 'Also the scripture says, "Do not put the Lord your God to the test." ' "

Brothers and sisters, this is the *spiritual temptation*. Can you imagine? Here the devil is using the Bible! He quotes textually from the Scripture. The devil also knows how to handle God's Word and cites texts with ease.

We have seen how the devil progressively dealt with Jesus. He pricked his vanity, he challenged Jesus regarding his belief that he was the Son of God, and then the devil tempted him, assuring him that the Scriptures would uphold him if he did the devil's bidding! The devil was sly in his audacious attack. He put to the test the very spiritual framework on which Jesus' faith, wisdom, and loving service hung.

With the devil putting the Bible on the table for discussion, the Lord with the same Bible met the test and showed in full measure the true stature of the Son of God:

" 'Also the scripture says, Do not put the Lord your God to the test.' " The devil's approach in this temptation is one that we also use many times to prove that we are Christians, pristine Christians, the best in the community, in the country, or in the world. This temptation comes to me also, to build my ego: "I am the best pastor; the other pastors fall short. I am a perfect Christian, because the others do not measure up." Often this pride is inflated by the assumption that the individual is more facile in handling Scripture, more correct in interpretation, absolutely inerrant in all teaching. Out of such a temptation comes a competitive and individualistic spirit: "Look at him over there! What a disgrace! Abandoned by God, because he is not as I am, a pastor shining in all the brightness of Scripture and a servant of God."

That temptation comes to the whole church when it says: "The other churches are not quite up to speed. We are the only true church." We have to be careful in this matter, my beloved. Let us remember that the Scripture also says: "Not everyone who says to me, 'Lord, Lord,' will enter the kingdom of heaven" (Matt. 7:21). Many people talk about the Word of God, but they do not put it into practice, not in their human relations, not in their social responsibilities, not in their spiritual lives. For that reason the gospel, beyond the mere words, puts emphasis on love and evidence in deeds. Hence it says: "You will know them by their fruits" (Matt. 7:16).

If we look again at the lesson in today's gospel, it is possible to conclude that speaking God's Word is not a sure guarantee for being a Christian. Satan is so deceptive that his disguise can suggest that everything is beautiful. He leaves the impression that he can do everything and that he makes everything easy. Just as we have said: "Luzbel" seems to be a "beautiful light," defusing the innocent to believe that he is the very God.

"Luzbel" appears attractive and eloquent, as if he possessed the truth, offered the way of life, and with subtle seduction invites us to share in his temptation: "I will give you everything and you will be happy."

Brothers and sisters, our Lord Jesus Christ suffered all these temptations and conquered them during the forty days in the desert. In truth, no one can withstand temptations. Not the best pastor, not the best priest, not the best bishop, not the very pope himself, with all his fame for holiness, can conquer temptations.

The only one who can triumph over the devil's slick assaults is Jesus Christ. For that reason, above all, we need him! For that reason, when the Spirit of God is with us, when we plead to come into communion with Christ Jesus, yes! then alone we are able to pass Satan's testing, in the hour of temptation, because then I am not *only* Medardo, and you are not *only* you, but Christ is with you and with me. God is within us!

When we are with God, then we are the winners. Our riches and our power are found when Christ is in us, because in that way we shall conquer all temptations and receive through him the gift of life. Both our conscience and our very being, the gift of God, will overflow with joy, because we have done his will.

SO MAY IT BE.

65

5

JESUS CHRIST IS
THE HISTORY
OF SALVATION

HOMILY
For the Second Sunday in Lent

LESSONS:

Jer. 26:8-15
Phil. 3:17–4:1
Luke 13:31-35

At that very hour some Pharisees came and said to him [Jesus], "Get away from here, for Herod wants to kill you."
He said to them,
"Go and tell that fox for me, 'Listen, I am casting out demons and performing cures today and tomorrow, and on the third day I finish my work. Yet today, tomorrow, and the next day I must be

on my way, because it is impossible for a prophet to be killed outside of Jerusalem.'

"Jerusalem, Jerusalem, the city that kills the prophets and stones those who are sent to it! How often have I desired to gather your children together as a hen gathers her brood under her wings, and you were not willing! See, your house is left to you. And I tell you, you will not see me until the time comes when you say, 'Blessed is the one who comes in the name of the Lord'" (Luke 13:31-35).

5

JESUS CHRIST IS THE HISTORY OF

SALVATION

Introduction

Brothers and sisters: The holy gospel which was just read points out that Jesus, as an individual, this Jesus of Jerusalem, had become a controversial figure. Many things were said about him. Some were of the opinion that he was becoming an agitator among the people. Others were sure that he opposed Caesar because of political questions. Others maintained that he was teaching the people not to obey the Mosaic laws, thus overturning the basic foundation of their faith. Others criticized him for being a glutton. Others accused him of overdrinking. It was coming to the point where he was considered dangerous, stigmatized as seditious.

However, there were always people who found truth in Christ. They accepted and received him as the Son of God. Those believers, who at that time recognized him as the Son of God, could testify that in reality Jesus was no agitator, but that truly he was a person of love, radiating compassion, mercy, and kindness. Only because of that love which he incarnated was he able to speak against all that was not good for the world and humanity.

Jesus was a very popular person. Those who had caught his full historic and divine dimension, evident for them in his message, followed him with great hope. They recognized him as God, the Savior, the promised Messiah. Even among those who were not his friends, for example the Pharisees who were his declared enemies, there were many who admired him and were convinced that he certainly was the Son of God.

These Pharisees, who belonged to the ruling class, had their ears open to everything that was being said and were also informed about government affairs. Through contacts with Herod they realized early that the evil king and his henchmen had decided to kill Jesus and had made secret plans. But when that scheme was hatched, some of those Pharisees who were sympathetic toward Jesus and respected his cause happened to be present. Once in the know about this treachery, they lost no time in going to tell Jesus.

Jesus' Reactions When Faced by Threats

When these Pharisees reached Jesus, they said: "Get away from here, for Herod wants to kill you." When Jesus heard about this death sentence, his reply was quick and final: "Go and tell that fox for me that I have to do my work, I have to complete my mission, including my going to Jerusalem, because I must die in Jerusalem. It is impossible for a prophet to die outside of Jerusalem."

This reaction of Jesus demonstrated great dignity because it confronted the situation, making it clear that "Herod, as governor, has to understand that I have to complete my mission which has been given me, that I have to do my work of healing the sick, of expelling the demons, and I have to go to Jerusalem, even though there they are going to kill me. But that is my destiny; that is the history of salvation which I have come to write: that I, as the Son of God, die in Jerusalem."

That was Jesus' human reaction. But immediately following we find in this posture something very divine. I can imagine Jesus, sensing the paradox: the deceptive and failed lives of the crowd around him, to whom he wished to give true life, and at the same time, the plotting of that very world which wanted to kill him. He knew that some did not recognize him as the Son of God. Yet, for example, the very governor, who wanted to kill him, was a child of God; God loved him too, even though he was carefully planning to kill Jesus. Face to face with this crumbling human condition, the

70

Lord was filled with a deep sadness and began to cry. In his sorrow he expressed and affirmed in the following words the sweet depth of his divine love and the lofty heights of his humanity: "Jerusalem, Jerusalem, the city that kills the prophets and stones those who are sent to it! How often have I desired to gather your children together as a hen gathers her brood under her wings, and you were not willing!"

The World's Reaction to the Love of Jesus

That, lamentably, is the reaction of the world regarding God's work. We must recognize, brothers and sisters, that many children of God, sent by God, have come, bearing the truth in their hands, proclaiming the new kingdom in the name of the Lord, and the world has not recognized them. But it has threatened them, reviled them, imprisoned them, and killed them while persecuting the church. For that very reason the holy gospel states, and listen well: "Now that you have killed all those whom God has sent you and have not wanted to recognize them, behold, I have left your house deserted; your house will remain deserted."

My beloved, as you ponder this gospel, I tell you that it left me very heavy of heart, very ashamed, because we must recognize that many of the terrible things that are happening here in our country are in part because Salvadorans have failed also to recognize those who were the children of God. Have they not killed unjustly those who were innocent, who were children of God? In the same way we have sinned, as those who did not receive the Lord Jesus Christ himself, who did not recognize him and embrace him as the Son of God. Yet the Lord continues to send others and the world, tangled up in its sin, does not recognize them. For that reason at the end of the gospel it says: "And I tell you, you will not see me again, you will not see love, you will not see peace, you will not see the glory of the Lord until that time comes when you say: 'Blessed is the one who comes in the name of the Lord.'"

Those Who Come in the Name of the Lord

BROTHERS AND SISTERS: As the people of God, we have to recognize those whom the Lord sends. We must ask the Holy Spirit to help us to know, to help us to discover the true children of God. Then, as the church of Jesus Christ, we can light the way and correctly guide our people. Also we must ask God for pardon. We need his pardon because, as a society, as the world of El Salvador, we have committed the great sin of stoning, threatening, and killing the true servants of God. Let us remember what the Lord says, that not until we learn to discern whom he sends, shall we be able to see him. That occurs when we live in full recognition of Christ as the blessed one who comes in the name of the Lord.

Brothers and sisters, let us all be converted into "little Christs," God's children, and let us go and serve, helping our people, because every one of us has to fulfill his or her destiny, each with our own mission. Jesus was obedient. See how he reacts before those who warned him that some plotted to kill him. They told him: "Get away from here, for Herod wants to kill you." His answer sealed his divine character: he had to fulfill, he had to complete his divine sacrificial act of love for all humanity. In that way, impelled by divine love, our church also has to do God's will.

Let us all together ask the Lord to help us find the knowledge and wisdom to discover what God wants of us. Where do we see him in our midst? Where is God showing himself to us? By whom is he made manifest? We become aware when we reach that point where we discover that the expression "Blessed is the one who comes in the name of the Lord" truly finds fulfillment in us. Then, and only then, shall we have the opportunity to live, worthy of the kingdom of God. But that will only happen when we learn to discover, as Christ did, the gracious and good will of our true Father.

May the peace of God be with all of us.

6

JESUS CHRIST GIVES US HIS FRIENDSHIP IN THE GOSPEL

HOMILY
For the Fifth Sunday after the Resurrection

LESSONS:

Acts 11:19-30
1 John 4:1-11
John 15:7-17

If you abide in me, and my words abide in you, ask for whatever you wish, and it will be done for you. My Father is glorified by this, that you bear much fruit and become my disciples. As the Father has loved me, so have I loved you; abide in my love. If you keep my commandments, you will abide in my love, just as I have kept my Father's commandments and abide in his love.

I have said these things to you so that my joy may be in you, and that your joy may be complete. This is my commandment, that you love one another as I have loved you. No one has greater love than this, to lay down one's life for one's friends. You are my friends if you do what I command you. I do not call you servants any longer, because the servant does not know what the master is doing; but I have called you friends, because I have made known to you everything that I have heard from my Father. You did not choose me but I chose you. And I appointed you to go and bear fruit, fruit that will last, so that the Father will give you whatever you ask him in my name. I am giving you these commands so that you may love one another (John 15:7-17).

6

JESUS CHRIST GIVES US HIS FRIENDSHIP

IN THE GOSPEL

Introduction

Brothers and sisters: I do not believe that a great deal of explanation is necessary to understand that, according to the gospel, the most important element for unity is love. And vice versa. It is love that preserves unity, and in order that there may be love, it is necessary that unity be preserved, such unity grounded in knowing Christ as a divine, world-encompassing, very human and social being.

God does not speak to us in philosophical categories that we cannot understand. Jesus Christ speaks to us very clearly about what we know of our own lives, because the gospel is life. The gospel proclaims the message of God in our lives, the good news that he is with us in good days and bad. In the midst of our joy, our happiness, our sufferings, and our sadness he is always with us.

Let us think, for a moment, about one aspect of love. For example, when we are married to another person, we learn to love him or her. If sometimes that person is absent, we feel a loss as final as death. We suffer much because this loved one is not with us. That bond of togetherness has produced a special feeling that is called love. Only when we communicate, when we are together and enjoy a normal relationship, can we grow in love.

The Weak Friend and the Strong Friend

One time there were two men: one of them was very weak, so weak, that whenever faced by any problem or caught off guard, he turned to his vices. Unless he found an escape, he was consumed by despair and anxiety. His life was sad, because he could not withstand the least testing. He easily caved in whenever he was faced by circumstances that depressed him. He was too fragile as a person to cope with the slightest problem without going overboard, drowning himself in mind-dumbing dissipation. If there was no escape in alcohol or other drugs, his suffering was unbearable. He cried and despaired, sure that the whole world had abandoned him. In such self-torture he tried to live.

But one day he and another man became friends and this friend loved him. The concern and sympathetic attitude of this new friend, his appreciation and esteem for the weaker man, were so assuring that the weaker man felt strengthened by the stronger one. This new ally brought moral fiber. With his love he gave support, and that offered him such security and trust that the weak friend changed completely. He began to find meaning in life; no longer did he need to escape through his vices.

Protected by the love of his friend, he made progress and reached heights that alone he never could have realized before. The affection of his friend so renewed his life that in an extraordinary fashion he began to dream of a new vision for life. But unfortunately, the day came when the weak friend had to move to another place, and he lost his benefactor. Now he no longer had this buffer of friendship that always afforded positive advice. When that friend who helped him, that friend who uplifted him, that friend who assured him with words of love and encouragement was no longer there, the unfortunate man in his weakness fell again into his habits and returned to his former state of self-destruction. Lower and lower he fell, because he missed the strength of that friend.

God Is Our Strong Friend

I want to tell you, brothers and sisters, that the weak man, that fragile person about whom we have been speaking, in reality is all

76

of us because we all are sinners. And the strong friend is God, the only one who can free us from all guilt, for without his help we cannot keep on course in this life. Without his divine guidance we fall headlong into failure. Now more than ever we need his strength, his counsel and wisdom, so that each and every one of us, as individuals or as communities, may grow in the faith that will enable us to become a little more demanding and assertive in our commitment to unity, within that human family that is clothed anew with the Holy Spirit.

What need do we have for divine armor? Why is it so important that we count on the goodness of the Lord? Simply that we not be struck down by our problems, that we may be sure that we can count on his love to bless and to evaluate moments of hardship or anxiety fairly. He, then, is our security. He is our support, that strong friend and protector. He is the friend who never fails us.

For that reason, brothers and sisters, the Lord Jesus tells us in today's reading: "Abide in me; if you abide in me you will know that love. You will be able to love, and this is the commandment that I leave with you, that as my Father loves me, that you love each other. And in that love, you have not chosen me." He continues: "I have first chosen you, that you may have joy, that you may not suffer, that you may not walk confused in life, that in the midst of human and social problems, you may have me to whom you may cling through faith, love, and hope."

The message that the Scripture leaves with us is that we need not come to an evil end, not even when the uncertainties, the confusions, and the desperations of raw life threaten us with doubts about our existence as the Lord's creatures. We need not fall into the abyss of anxiety and affliction, not even in the worst circumstances that life's conditions may impose on us.

Illumined by Scripture we see that we have a strong friend, a powerful friend who is our mightiest supporter. To him we must cling and in him find strength, because God will never allow us to fall into the evil clutches of the devil.

God Reveals Himself to Those Who Cry Out to Him

Brothers and sisters: Our situation is aggravated by adversities and grave problems that are an arsenal of pain, violence, and despair. But thanks be to God there are sons and daughters who cry out to him and recognize him as their Savior, as the Father of him who gave his life for the forgiveness of our sins.

These sons and daughters who belong to him, who are "not ashamed of the gospel" (Rom. 1:16), have learned to understand that we can turn to that strong friend, our God, who reveals himself in the refugee camps and hospitals, and among those fleeing and being pursued. The good news is that we can seek him and that he can help us with his love, and we, in turn, can offer him our lives.

And what about the person who, unfortunately, is not a loyal and fervent friend of him to whom we, with generations of Christians, give testimony?

The gospel is clear in saying that the strong friend, embodying God's love, is the Holy Spirit, poured out over these his sons and daughters. Thus the Scripture is fulfilled: "that your joy may be complete, that you may have joy. No one has greater love than this, that he lay down his life for his friends. You are my friends if you do what I command you."

Love of God, Love of Mother

Within a few days we shall celebrate Mother's Day. I have already mentioned this several times, but now that this celebration is getting near, I want to repeat it: there is no other love on the face of this earth that is nearer to God's love than a mother's love.

A mother is the authentic representative of humanity at its best, the unique example of what truly is God's love, because she is the only human being who can sacrifice her life in giving life to her children. That is the love that we feel whenever our mother touches us. It seems that whatever hurt, whatever pain, regardless of its intensity, is lessened, because the mother herself feels the child's pain. She so identifies with the child that it is as if the circumstances are reversed. She absorbs her child's hurt because she feels it in the very core of her being. In this very human example, the mother wishes to make the pain that her child suffers her own, so as to free him or her from suffering. That love needs no special study at a university to comprehend it. This is the love we have felt on the part of our own parents, especially of our mothers, or other benefactors who have loved us as a real father or mother.

Now, understanding what the love of God is, the Lord tells us: "Let your love grow and increase, and not be derailed by whatever adversity life poses. Here in God's love you have my Spirit, my glorifying presence, and my companionship."

The same God says to us: "People of El Salvador, if you do not want violence and those problems undermining and tearing down you and your society, and throwing you even more off track and away from me, trust my word, my promise of the new kingdom. If you do not wish your present crisis eventually to produce a sickness that will spread to every part of your being, keep yourselves close to me in faith and trust. I am strong; I am your friend who will not fail you; I am he who truly wants to help you.

My Personal Testimony

This, brothers and sisters, is my personal testimony when I feel dispirited and weighed down with problems. Being human as I am, when I have to make some decision and find no answer, for me then there is no better medicine than the Spirit of the Lord. Immediately, I run to my friend, to God, and I go in prayer to tell him the problems that surround me. Then after such a talk with him, I feel myself strengthened.

A Final Reflection

BROTHERS AND SISTERS: Now that we live in the midst of these times that predict further conflicts, see here God's Word which reminds us that as children of our Lord we must not become divided. We must be fed on love itself in order to be edified and united in peace, by being with Christ. Only in that way shall we never be abandoned nor left alone, because God our Father will be with us. We must remain united around our strong friend, our Lord and Savior.

Whenever we feel forsaken and fear that we may weaken, whenever we find ourselves lost in despair and anxiety, let us seek God, our friend in Jesus Christ, let us tell him our problems and our deepest frustrations. After experiencing heartfelt communion with him, our loyal and strong friend, and after hearing his divine Word, which will become like living water, we will be refreshed in our innermost beings. Enraptured by his Spirit, we shall be able to show forth, with no boasting about our spirituality, that the joy of God is complete in each and every one of us. Amen.

The peace of God which surpasses all understanding, keep our hearts and our minds in Christ our Lord. SO MAY IT BE!

7

WALKING TOGETHER IS GIVING TESTIMONY TO JESUS CHRIST

HOMILY
For the Sixth Sunday after the Resurrection

LESSONS:

Acts 1:15-26
1 John 4:13-21
John 17:11-19

And now I am no longer in the world, but they are in the world, and I am coming to you. Holy Father, protect them in your name that you have given me, so that they may be one, as we are one. While I was with them, I protected them in your name that you have given me. I guarded them, and not one of them was lost except the one destined to be lost, so that the Scripture might be fulfilled.

But now I am coming to you, and I speak these things in the world so that they may have my joy made complete in themselves. I have given them your word, and the world has hated them because they do not belong to the world, just as I do not belong to the world. I am not asking you to take them out of the world, but I ask you to protect them from the evil one. They do not belong to the world, just as I do not belong to the world. Sanctify them in the truth; your word is truth. As you have sent me into the world, so I have sent them into the world. And for their sakes I sanctify myself, so that they also may be sanctified in truth (John 17:11-19).

7

WALKING TOGETHER IS GIVING

TESTIMONY TO JESUS CHRIST

Introduction

Brothers and sisters: My pleasure in speaking to you today is heightened because of the occasion, the celebration of Mother's Day. This allows me to share with you what is especially significant for this day.

We pray that God may help us, you as much as me, to speak from God's holy Word. May the grace of the Lord Jesus Christ be with all of us.

The holy gospel speaks to us about the unity of Christians and gives us the example of our Lord Jesus Christ, in that he and his Father are *one*. The gospel tells us of the love of Jesus who, as our brother and friend, is concerned about us and intercedes before God, our Father, on our behalf. Jesus Christ wants all Christians to be united, that we may form one body and, together, become *one*, even as that unity of love is forged in God, the Father, Jesus, and the Holy Spirit.

Our spirits become alive as we sing: "Together, as brothers, we travel to meet the Lord." This reminds me that today a group of Christian sisters of diverse nationalities are visiting our country. Their stated reason is to seek peace in the world, and to that end they decided to leave their homes and travel throughout the world, pleading and contending for peace. And they have asked us also to work for peace in the world, especially in our country of El Salvador. We join together with them in their petition during this worship service.

This helps us to recognize that we are not alone on our journey with the Lord. He makes himself known and we find him on all sides of the planet. This witnesses to the solidarity that we have with our brothers and sisters who come from other countries in the Lord's name. We are not alone in spite of geographic distances and borders that divide us or differences in customs in each country. The Lord boosts our spirits, assuring us that we are not alone, that in other places there also are those who struggle to find that peace which we desire, working to realize such unity where there are no differences, where we all are *one,* even as Christ and his Father are *one.*

God Comforts Us as a Mother

Today is Mother's Day, a day celebrated in various countries to recognize and compare, possibly, a mother's love with God's love. But I ask myself: "What purposes are served by this celebration? Will it recognize a mother's love, comparing it to that of God's? Will it recognize the role that a true mother must fulfill? Will it be an expression of gratitude for the gift of life, or merely a promotional opportunity for businesses?"

This celebration should have objectives that are ethical and religious in character in order to praise the true value of mothers. If we wish to compare a mother's love with God's love, we find that the Bible, Isaiah 66:13, gives us God's promise: "As a mother comforts her child, so I will comfort you."

The Objectives of Mother's Day

Here we are relating God's love to that of a mother, which means being wary of all kinds of questionable manipulations exploited in the celebration of this day dedicated to mothers.

I was mentioning to you the mother's importance to society, since the future society will take its shape from the child that she molds. From this perspective, the mother's role involves an entire generation, since she is responsible for the education of her children.

If in the home, for example, solid foundations are not laid and new positive values not imprinted on formative minds, but rather attitudes are nurtured by conflict, abuse, lies, and envy, such will be harvested in our children. That will be the model passed on to our future society.

We all, together, create the foundation for the families of society, but the mother is principally responsible because of her glorious role in bestowing life itself. It is true that not only the mother is the foundation of the social world, but, as I already said, in this instance we are not adopting her in a generic sense, but as the ideal that makes life a concrete reality with its potentials and capacities for both men and women.

This celebration, then, has many objectives. But one of the most important is to reflect on God's Word with respect to mothers as the seedbeds, the initiators of the family, the molders of social beings. According to God's commandment, the Christian's ideal has this objective: "to walk together so that a good society may evolve." The gospel tells us about this concern on the part of Jesus Christ, who for our benefit becomes one of us who are his children in this world. We see how Jesus, with love, implores his heavenly Father for that crown of blessings: "Holy Father, take care of us through the power of your name, the name that you have given me, that they may be completely united, as you and I."

To Walk Together Is to Be One

Brothers and sisters: We have to come together; men and women, we have to walk together—together in the home, together in work, together for social betterment, together in the church. Elbow to elbow, we will attain a world of peace, of love, and of justice.

Just as the Father and the Son are *one,* so also men and women, organizations and communities—we have to walk together, to give testimony that Jesus was sent into the world in the name of his Father, our God.

If we do not walk together, brothers and sisters, we are not witnessing that Jesus was sent to protect his children. He did not come wishing to take us out of the world, but to save us from the evil one. Thus it is a Christian virtue to walk together in solidarity without weakening ourselves over secondary differences. Brothers and sisters, if we walk together in this spirit, we shall be dedicating ourselves by our lives to Jesus, proclaiming in practice a gospel for peace on earth. That, indeed, is the teaching of Jesus, when he tells us that he has come to identify with us and implant within us that potential for complete joy, actualized only in him.

We are witnesses to that presence of unity among Christians in Jesus Christ. Our prayer today, as God's servants and Jesus' friends, will be to ask the Father for a genuine unity, sincere and open. We must pray for a world of peace for our children, for a different society in which they may learn to walk together and work together in the building of the new kingdom. We ask him to enable our sons and daughters to go hand in hand into a world of peace with justice and liberty. Our children are God's creation; for that reason the Lord does not want this generation to destroy them through injustice, violence, and war.

For all Christians, this worship service offers an opportunity to express true gratitude for the love of mothers and for the love of God. And if the present situation opens up the opportunity for our children to enjoy a reign of real peace, we could consecrate that realization of a national plan of salvation to the Father and the Lord Jesus Christ! But the sad part of our world is that our children celebrate this day in the midst of war.

A World of Peace for Our Children

BROTHERS AND SISTERS: Our prayer has to be a plea for our children. They are Jesus' concern. On their behalf, then, we must dedicate ourselves to uphold truth. In this way we also are witnessing to that to which the gospel testifies, that is, Jesus prayed that his disciples might be *one,* that they might have no differences or that these be overcome by compassion, pardon, and love. When we are *one,* many problems and disagreements are avoided; when we are divided, we give place to the evil one or we permit him to manipulate us.

86

Jesus prays for those who are in the world, to the end that we, as men and women, may be *one* in whatever way we form communities. And this commitment to unity is the greatest responsibility for the church community, for us Christians with an ecumenical spirit. If there is no unity among Christians, the reality of Jesus Christ's presence is denied and no truth emanates from the Father for this world.

Division Means War

BROTHERS AND SISTERS: What divides, what ends in meaningless discussions, and what results from power politics only bring war as its consequence. For that reason, children, obey your parents in everything, because this pleases the Lord. Parents, do not anger your children that they become discouraged or sidetracked onto the broad path of evil. Our children depend on us to sow in them the seeds of love for a life that wants to walk in harmony with others.

The Lord is wise, when he compares God's love with a mother's love. He says to us: "Can a woman forget her nursing child, or show no compassion for the child of her womb? Even these may forget, yet I will not forget you" (Isa. 49:15).

Those words from Isaiah are teaching us that it is true that a mother's love is like God's love, but at times—many times!—whether men or women, we fail to fulfill this human responsibility that has a divine dimension. But the Lord is always gracious and wise. For that reason his promise holds: "If some time a mother may forget her son, I will never forget him."

Final Reflection

BROTHERS AND SISTERS: There has to be a peaceful world. Unity among us has to begin by understanding ourselves, by being brotherly in our criticism and also by practicing self-criticism. Understand that both men and women are important in building the new kingdom. Between both human genders a communal unity must be formed, fundamental for society and its process of development. Only united in that way shall we fulfill the mission and the commitment that, as

Christians, we have with respect to our country, which, in the final analysis, means our own children.

May this be the message for now, as we celebrate Mother's Day here in this church. The future society for our children depends on us. Ours is a task that never ends; it is a battle that never ceases, but which must continue throughout all the days in which God gives us life, while he accompanies us and gives us his blessing. SO MAY IT BE!

8

THE HOLY SPIRIT
UNITES CHRISTIANS
IN JOY

HOMILY
For Pentecost Sunday

LESSONS:

Ezek. 37:1-14
Acts 2:1-21
John 7:37-39

On the last day of the festival, the great day, while Jesus was standing there, he cried out,

"Let anyone who is thirsty come to me, and let the one who believes in me drink. As the scripture has said, 'Out of the believer's heart shall flow rivers of living water.'"

Now he said this about the Spirit, which believers in him were to receive; for as yet there was no Spirit, because Jesus was not yet glorified (John 7:37-39).

89

8

THE HOLY SPIRIT UNITES

CHRISTIANS IN JOY

Introduction

Brothers and sisters: In Jerusalem there were three great religious festivals, very solemn, full of tradition and rich in religious meaning, and celebrated with great joy. These festivals included all the people. It is obvious that no one missed participating in these three special festivities.

The first of them was the Passover about which all of us know. The second festival was that of Tabernacles and the third, that of Pentecost.

When Jesus cried out in today's reading: "Let anyone who is thirsty come to me, and let the one who believes in me drink," he was at the Feast of Tabernacles, which was also called the Feast of Booths or of the Harvest.

That celebration had a double significance. First, it was historic. For that reason it was also called the Feast of Booths, because it recalled how God's chosen people had wandered in the wilderness and had to make provisional "booths" out of boughs for shelter. In keeping with that historic experience, the Feast of Tabernacles was celebrated by living in booths so that these descendants of wanderers in the wilderness would never forget how to be a suffering people on pilgrimage. Such an annual event would reinforce the memory, that by enduring all kinds of weather, hunger, thirst, and all the other difficulties as a consequence of their pilgrim wanderings, God always stood at their side. Fully conscious of this historic significance, Jesus was present on the most important day of the festival.

The second purpose of the festival was to give thanks. It was a feast to celebrate the ingathering of the fruits and grains and to thank God for the harvest just completed. To this was added an obligation that those who had a bountiful harvest should share what exceeded their need with those who had not produced enough. It was a commitment for the rich to share with the poor. Without a doubt, that was a custom worthy of note!

For the celebration of this phase of the festival, the people came together and brought that portion of their harvest to be given to the priest, that he might distribute it to the community, sharing with those who, although they had worked, had not reaped a sufficient amount. This was a beautiful festival, a very symbolic feast of brotherhood of great importance. For here was recognized the interdependence of all humanity.

The Rite of Tabernacles

As part of this festival there was another very important rite. The priest led a procession, much like the entry of those of us officiating in our worship today. The priest with his assistants carried jars, filled with water fresh from the spring, and proceeded to the Lord's altar. The jars with the fresh water symbolized that God is the God of life and recalled that God was with his people who were dying of thirst in the desert. There from the rock he brought forth water, sufficient to give life and restore his people, saving them from death and thus enabling them to continue onward.

In this ceremony, as the priest and his assistants were offering the jars filled with water, Jesus stood up at that very moment before the people and cried out what we heard in the gospel reading: "Let anyone who is thirsty come to me, and let the one who believes in me drink."

The Thirst of Our People

BROTHERS AND SISTERS: These words must resonate deep within us, as Salvadoran Christians, since they echo our feelings, those within

92

our innermost beings, because the present conditions in which we live in our society and its political history have made us a people even more thirsty! Only our jars are filled with needs and problems. As a result, the church stays close to the believers and with Jesus it exclaims: "Let anyone who is thirsty come to me, and let the one who believes in me drink."

When I thought about this thirst that our people suffer, I realized how sad it was to see that there even exists among our masses a thirst for vengeance, for hate, for murder. It is sad to reflect on the social and economic reality of our country, knowing that in addition to the negative, there is a thirst for justice, for improved labor conditions, for better health, for more education, the absence of all which represents another face of death. But God in his mercy does not want such life-threatening thirst to increase, because God is not the God of death; he is the God of life. He does not wish to give his assent to a journey toward death, nor wish to accompany anyone on such a losing venture, on the path where life is lost.

Our God is a God who wishes to help us find ourselves, to illuminate that path by which we will find life in abundance. We will follow our God as our guide to be filled with life. We will discover for ourselves through him a genuine sense of security. To those of us who are broken in heart and who conscientiously seek a community that frees and saves us, the Lord exclaims: "Let anyone who is thirsty come to me, and let the one who believes in me drink." To fulfill that mission the church must also reconsider its way of creating God's family in light of its Christian responsibility.

As our teacher, Jesus finds his answer to this challenge in these words, spoken by the prophet Isaiah: "The Lord will guide you continually, and satisfy your needs in parched places, and make your bones strong; and you shall be like a watered garden, like a spring of water, whose waters never fail" (Isa. 58:11).

The Festival of Pentecost

Today the church celebrates the Festival of Pentecost, another of the three great historic religious festivals. The reading that we just heard from Acts speaks of this. As we know, the first disciples, the first Christians, had received Jesus' promise of the coming of the Holy Spirit, but until now they had not experienced his promised presence. It was not until the Festival of Pentecost that the apostles received the Spirit, promised by Jesus, as their pastor.

This happened precisely at a moment when all the apostles were together in one place. Note how the Scripture emphasizes this occasion to the point of seeming redundant. The book of Acts begins by relating how all were *together* and *of the same mind*. This repetition is intentional, that we may understand that it was when the first Christians were *united, together, of one mind,* that this special phenomenon happened, this divine act by which the Holy Spirit was poured out on the apostles.

Then the Word of God became alive and the promise of Jesus was fulfilled. On the one hand, that which had been announced by the prophet Joel was completed: "In the last days it will be, God declares, that I will pour out my Spirit upon all flesh . . ." (Acts 2:17). And on the other, there was astonishment and excitement on the part of the believers, for then, filled with the Holy Spirit, they were convinced once again that it was Jesus Christ who was manifesting himself by revealing this truth. The Christian movement was at once transfused with vigorous life and great joy. What followed seems quite strange, for there at this extraordinary occurrence the Christian movement suddenly became universal, reaching to the farthest ends of the world; it then became the church of Jesus Christ. Even the Jews who had come from regions of that area and other parts of the world for the celebration of this God-inspired happening were surprised because the apostles were speaking in their own dialects and languages. These believers in Jesus were being reclothed (Col. 3:10) by the Holy Spirit, proclaiming themselves to be the founders of the church and initiating the proclamation of the gospel. The tongues of fire on the disciples' heads, like bishops' miters, were as awe-inspiring as the words that were spoken to those who had come from afar to Jerusalem. They recognized their own languages as spoken by those men from Galilee, and they began to understand what the disciples were saying. The unique thing is that these people came from Crete, Pamphylia, Mesopotamia, Egypt, and all parts of the world. However, they all understood what the apostles were saying about baptism, about the gospel that they proclaimed, and about the plan of salvation that was to be announced throughout the world until the end of time.

Pentecost Announces Unity

When the Holy Spirit is poured out on the church, on the people of God, he produces that phenomenon which is Pentecost, what we, as Christians, many times do not want to accept. That is, that as Christians we should live together, within the worldwide borders of the churches that speak as God's prophetic voices. As Christians, we can work together and be together and unite in our mutual objectives of worship and service. Pentecost is the festival that must be remembered permanently in the church, since it offers the Spirit's joy and enthusiasm to move us to bring the church spiritually together. The earthly organization of the church is necessary to complete the mission that Jesus commended to us in his message in the synagogue in Nazareth (Luke 4:18-19).

The Cold Church

Whenever a church is a cold community, one that neither prays nor works on behalf of the neighbor; whenever a church is too negligent regarding problems and misunderstandings and lacks the courage and good intention to face the issues and find solutions, then we must ask for the Holy Spirit to be present, because he alone can bring light on the matter and put our lives on the good road toward unity. It is the Holy Spirit who gives joy to our hearts. For this we worship him, happy to know that with him we feel the presence of God in our midst.

I am sure that with this kind of worship, this kind of inspired and lived religion, we will never leave our worship services bored at not having our faith revitalized. We are not going to leave discouraged; instead we are going to leave satisfied with our spirits lifted

95

up, ready to face life, because God goes within our souls. The Holy Spirit is present within human beings just as we heard in the example from the Old Testament. God gave life back to dry bones, making human beings again with flesh and blood. That is what the Holy Spirit does. That is what the Holy Spirit means for believers. It is more than joining bones together to form the skeleton, filling it out with flesh and tendons, then covering it with skin. God gives dead bones the breath of life that they might be revived as living beings.

That is a picture of what we are, as sinners. We are just like those dry bones, inert. That is what Christians are without faith, like that cold church that does not demonstrate a living gospel witness and a sense of oneness, of being the community of Christ's church. The Holy Spirit is the one who gives back to us the breath of life, he fills us with grace and he empowers us to become living witnesses in the world. That is why we must invoke his presence to strengthen our faith that our Christian testimony may help to solidify the religious foundation of our community and thus convert a cold church into a church that shows Christ incarnated in his people, into a church like that of the apostles which becomes a concrete historic reality within today's world.

I, as a Christian without the Holy Spirit, do not serve nor sense the presence of Jesus. But when the Holy Spirit is with me, I feel the presence of God who inspires me and moves me to serve my neighbors. When the Spirit of the Lord is with all of us, we are a congregation, both strong and blessed by God's love. When the Holy Spirit is over his church, then it is an apostolic church; it is bearing the gospel and it is living its history. It is actively engaged in Christ's plan of salvation by becoming an active church in service, dynamic and involved. It is transformed into a united church that, in spite of whatever problems or differences might exist, is able—now, as a congregation of God's children, *united* and *of one mind*—to worship and serve the Lord in his work of salvation, of liberating an enslaved world.

A Final Reflection

BROTHERS AND SISTERS: Pentecost must move us to pray because now is the moment, the opportune time when I want to invite you to ask our Lord Jesus Christ that our congregation may become a church, constant in worship. May our prayers become a deeply spiritual communication that responds to our faith, as we confront history in the social and political world in which we live.

It is prayer that will keep us together. It will help us to remain in communion with God and convert us into Christians, active and faithful to the gospel of our Lord Jesus Christ. It is such prayer that gives us positive thoughts and inspires us to understand everything in the best light.

Without the Holy Spirit we will have the problem of not being identified as truly Christian. We are never going to see the good in other people or in the organizations within our society, least of all in our brothers and sisters. We are always going to be thinking about their defects and broadcasting their deficiencies. Without the Holy Spirit our lives will not demonstrate honest justice and love. Apart from him, we will be corroded by selfishness that destroys us and voids our virtues. Without the Holy Spirit we will never be able to accept, help, or share with a brother or sister, because the Spirit is the one who turns on the light and illumines our consciences and sensitivities. Only with him can we see another human being without prejudice. Only then do we begin to comprehend the other, without gloating at blemishes or waiting for the earliest moment to cause hurt.

The Holy Spirit moves us to join with our brothers and sisters in order to bring all Christians together, inspired to clasp hands with Jesus Christ and work for his plan of salvation for all humanity. Only he can convert us into that one united body which is Jesus himself, incarnate in our history. Only then shall we be, all of us, that *one* which Jesus wanted us to be as Christians. Then we shall become those springs of living water which is life itself, knowing that God is with us. That is the life which we share, one with another, just as God in that new commandment, communicated to us by his elected one, his only Son, whose words we are to ponder: "To love one another" in the joy of his Spirit.

97

May the peace of God
which surpasses all understanding
keep your hearts and your minds
in Christ Jesus,
our Lord.
AMEN.

9

JESUS CHRIST IS THE CONSCIENCE FOR COMMUNAL ACTION

HOMILY
For the Third Sunday after Pentecost

LESSONS:

Gen. 3:9-15
2 Cor. 4:13-18
Mark 3:20-35

Then he [Jesus] went home; and the crowd came together again, so that they could not even eat. When his family heard it, they went out to restrain him, for people were saying, "He has gone out of his mind."

And the scribes who came down from Jerusalem said, "He has Beelzebul, and by the ruler of the demons he casts out demons."

And he called them to him, and spoke to them in parables, "How can Satan cast out Satan?

"If a kingdom is divided against itself, that kingdom cannot stand. And if a house is divided against itself, that house will not be able to stand.

"And if Satan has risen up against himself and is divided, he cannot stand, but his end has come.

"But no one can enter a strong man's house and plunder his property without first tying up the strong man; then indeed the house can be plundered.

"Truly I tell you, people will be forgiven for their sins and whatever blasphemies they utter; but whoever blasphemes against the Holy Spirit can never have forgiveness, but is guilty of an eternal sin"—for they had said, "He has an unclean spirit."

Then his mother and his brothers came; and standing outside, they sent to him and called him. A crowd was sitting around him; and they said to him,

"Your mother and your brothers and sisters are outside, asking for you." And he replied,

"Who are my mother and my brothers?" And looking at those who sat around him, he said,

"Here are my mother and my brothers! Whoever does the will of God is my brother and sister and mother" (Mark 3:20-35).

9

JESUS CHRIST IS THE CONSCIENCE

FOR COMMUNAL ACTION

Introduction

Brothers and sisters: As one recalls the conditions in which Jesus and his disciples lived when their ministry began, it was an environment similar to our own: much sickness, great physical and spiritual needs, rampant injustice, and numerous violations of human rights. Great political instability existed with armed groups rising in the mountains, and the people enduring uncertainties because of the burden of taxes and other laws imposed by the empire and local authorities. The people clammered for relief such as better living conditions, but only corruption, hunger, and abuse of the poor continued.

In the midst of that situation, so filled with tension and fear because of a regime that marginalized and oppressed the people, there appeared the charismatic figure of Jesus. He brought a message of life, of love, and of hope, and he assured this promise merely by asking for their trust. He did not dodge the issues, but communicated the meaning of trust with words as well as with his example and his deeds. As soon as he began to deal with the people, he became as one of them, especially the poor. It was an incarnation in which he identified with the specific problems of his followers. In that way, the mass of humanity that berated the crimes against individuals and society itself sought a savior. To that forgotten society he came as

Savior, understanding also their needs for spiritual food. They responded as a people pressed together by mutual misfortune, and crowded behind Jesus because they understood that this man brought a message of peace with justice and liberty. He brought a solution for all humanity's needs with the new kingdom that he announced and demonstrated with his deeds.

In his ministry Jesus gave concrete examples of his love by helping the people who followed him with acts of mercy and with an honest attitude that defended the interests of the poor. With them he accused the hypocrisy of the Pharisees and condemmed the hidden unfairness in the small print of the law. For that reason the number of those around him increased and his following grew wherever he went. They were so persistent that they did not even let him rest. He had to escape and retreat in order to communicate with God by prayer and to meditate about his mission.

The First Ones Chosen by the Lord

To prepare himself and carry out his task properly, Jesus picked twelve leaders to walk close to him and learn to put into practice what he taught.

These were the first to be chosen by the Lord. For them he found time and a place to be alone, to speak to them about the truths that must be shared. With these disciples he spoke of other things about which he felt they must be informed, but he suggested that they not speak of those things publicly right away. Let us remember that in the gospel we read repeatedly that expression: "But do not mention this to anyone." That which they shared together focused often on his divine mystery and also on the best way to deal with the crowds that gathered around him, awed by his presence. They analyzed among themselves what was occurring in each region in order better to communicate the Lord's message.

The Ministry of Faith and Service

Of course, later Jesus chose seventy more disciples, always with the usual mystery and methodology for continuing his ministry. As this missionary movement grew, so did public expectation; by then the authorities were troubled and wanted to oppress those who continued with their denunciations, demanding "freedom for the captives" and "liberty for the oppressed." The opposition was careful to note that those demanding change, like Jesus, identified with the poor. Nonetheless, Jesus and his followers continued to be involved with the current situation and moved from place to place to announce the good news of the Lord's gospel.

With that in mind Jesus always sent his disciples in twos, to care for each other and to reach more of the needy. Because they lived in dangerous times, it was unwise to travel alone. So these first believers went in twos for mutual support, but their faith was in the message that told of a ministry of love, combined with a spirit of service, touching as many of the suffering as possible.

As a result, the people were always surrounding Jesus, not even giving him time to eat. That is what today's gospel tells us. But Jesus had true compassion for those who followed and loved him. In contrast, he was stern and adamant with the hypocrites and condemned those who opposed the truth. In order to complete his mission he abandoned the banquet tables to call attention to those things that silence dared not hide. He left his food to care for the needy, to censure the sins of his contemporaries, and to teach about the new kingdom.

Jesus Stigmatized as Crazy and Satanic

We know by today's Scripture that some people were beginning to speak unfairly about Jesus, in the face of the people's public acclaim in seeking and identifying with him. Others, alone or in groups, entered the scene just to misinterpret him. They insinuated and accused him of being against the Roman Empire. Priests and Pharisees conspired against him because he tended to question their religious integrity. Due to Jesus' interpretation of God's Word, the authorities claimed that many people no longer respected the Sabbath. With no good intentions these enemies eventually began to ask among themselves, "What are we going to do with this man from Galilee?"

His family also began to worry, thinking: They are going to kill our loved one; they want to do away with Jesus, and the worst is that they are going to harm us also. Let us go and get him, so that we can rescue him. Because if they capture him, they are going to harm him and maybe us too. We will get him first and save him. If they take him, they may hurt him, even demanding the ultimate sacrifice.

Just like other exceptional people who have worked for love and justice and been stigmatized as crazy, so Jesus suffered the same fate, even branded by his own family. When they saw how he was totally committed to his mission, they came to the conclusion: Our Jesus is crazy. We will go and get him! With that purpose in mind his family went to bring him back home, because some said that he was crazy. How was it possible that his own loved ones would come to that conclusion? Perhaps the reality was that his mother and his brothers and sisters were asking themselves a different question: How is it possible that our Jesus, who is of such humble background, is risking his life to talk about these things and enter that dangerous arena, identifying himself with so many people? He should know better and keep his place!

And his enemies? What were they saying? They decided to come up with some way to put an end to him, since for them he was a very dangerous person. Up until then, they had been trying to invent a theological trap, dealing with Mosaic tradition. But now a new idea took form: the best way to destroy him was to say that he was given his power by Beelzebul, the chief of the devils, which enabled him to do all those marvelous things that the people admired and called "miracles."

At this juncture of today's gospel reading Jesus confronted two distinct dilemmas. What are they?

Perhaps both predicaments involve doubt, but he converted them into forceful lessons. The first deals with the question: "How can my family, my loved ones, presume that I am crazy? How is it that they cannot perceive the full dimension of my prophetic task?" His desire was to console them, but also to prepare them for his divine destiny, the cross, as we see from what follows.

Jesus Embraced Two Kinds of Community Equally

The gospel narrative continues with the family's arrival, where Jesus was surrounded by his apostles. One of them informed him that his mother, his brothers, and his sisters were eager to see him outside. Jesus took this opportunity to distinguish between the beautiful relationship of community, such as his followers, and that of family, both divinely instituted as functioning entities in society. He showed, by example, that at times one must renounce even those who are dearest to carry out the greater work of establishing God's justice in the wider community through dedication of self in building the new kingdom, the body of Christ, and carrying that divine mission to completion. He related the two kinds of community, that of family and that of his following, by asking: "Who are my mother and my brothers?" Then looking around at all his followers and at his disciples, he added: "Here are my mother and my brothers! Whoever does the will of God is my brother and sister and mother."

Jesus Condemned the Blasphemers

The second situation that gave him concern was the newly fabricated calumny of the Pharisees that he was in league with Beelzebul, the chief of devils. Here Jesus could not remain silent, for in the name of his Father he had to speak out. To counter that falsehood he called the teachers of the law to task for spreading such blasphemy. With divine wisdom Jesus deflated the arguments of those inflated religious professionals. Once again he proved his deeper perception of the sacred Word and his innate grace that enabled him to reveal the dishonesty that lay behind the arguments of the Pharisees and the teachers of the law.

With the underhanded maneuvering of his enemies, Jesus felt deeply hurt. They stooped to any depths to perpetuate injustice in the world, heaping slander on top of falsehoods that were quickly broadcast merely to secure their own manipulation of evil. But our Lord Jesus Christ, then and now, personifies truth, love, and faith, which in a situation such as this reveals the gospel, the good news, that he was strong and had the courage to speak with moral and religious authority against evil, against sin. As a result his condemnation of them was stinging: "Truly I tell you, people will be forgiven for their sins and whatever blasphemies they utter; but whoever blasphemes against the Holy Spirit can never have forgiveness, but is guilty of an eternal sin."

Christ Is the Community's Conscience

BROTHERS AND SISTERS: There are actually many persons and many institutions dedicated to human betterment and the defense of human rights. There are many churches who are serving the people, attentive to their cries and needs. These human institutions and religious communities identify with our people in the suffering and grief of the poor. In truth, we must be consciously alert that our involvement also comes from the heart, even if it takes us to the cross. All of our reactions to these problems are, in the end, motivated by the Holy Spirit. However, we do know that there are those who say that to bring help from this Christian perspective is not working in the spirit of Jesus Christ, but is "being a communist, being subversive."

A Final Reflection

I want to conclude, brothers and sisters, with this observation. Whenever we hear such criticism let us listen carefully, lest we permit such negativism to convince us and we fall into the trap that the Pharisees and teachers of the law were setting for Jesus. It is better to remember the warning of Jesus in his condemnation against unholy slander, equating communal actions of conscience in defense of the people's good with works of Beelzebul: "Truly I tell you, people will be forgiven for their sins . . . but whoever blasphemes against the Holy Spirit can never have forgiveness, but is guilty of an eternal sin."

That which serves to comfort us here is the motivation of the Holy Spirit that brings us to act and strengthens our faith. I must tell you the truth: it is a fact that, in the absence of bold reaction on the part of the faithful community to such a slanderous innuendo and its result, inaction in these times has caused many deaths and unforgettable torture. It is only natural and logical that when these humanitarian organizations and our churches are stigmatized as seditious, we are going to be afraid and sometimes affected.

As a consequence, it happens that friends and our families also are worried about our mission for justice, peace, and liberty. They ask us to change course, even tone down our gospel cause; to our response of faith and conviction they also say to us: "You are crazy. There is no doubt about it. You are not involved in a Christian ministry, but you are seeking other objectives. You are crazy, because you are never going to succeed!" At such a time, brothers and sisters, let us keep in mind, more than ever, the true meaning of the gospel for today. For my part, I tell them: "The Holy Spirit is present with us and is within us, since Christ is the conscience of the Christian community."

May the peace of God
which surpasses all understanding
keep our hearts and our minds
in Jesus Christ,
our Lord.
AMEN.